TALES OF MYSTERY AND IMAGINATION

The *Oxford Progressive English Reader*s series provides a wide range of reading for learners of English.

Each book in the series has been written to follow the strict guidelines of a syllabus, wordlist and structure list. The texts are graded according to these guidelines; Grade 1 at a 1,400 word level, Grade 2 at a 2,100 word level, Grade 3 at a 3,100 word level, Grade 4 at a 3,700 word level and Grade 5 at a 5,000 word level.

The latest methods of text analysis, using specially designed software, ensure that readability is carefully controlled at every level. Any new words which are vital to the mood and style of the story are explained within the text, and reoccur throughout for maximum reinforcement. New language items are also clarified by attractive illustrations.

Each book has a short section containing carefully graded exercises and controlled activities, which test both global and specific understanding.

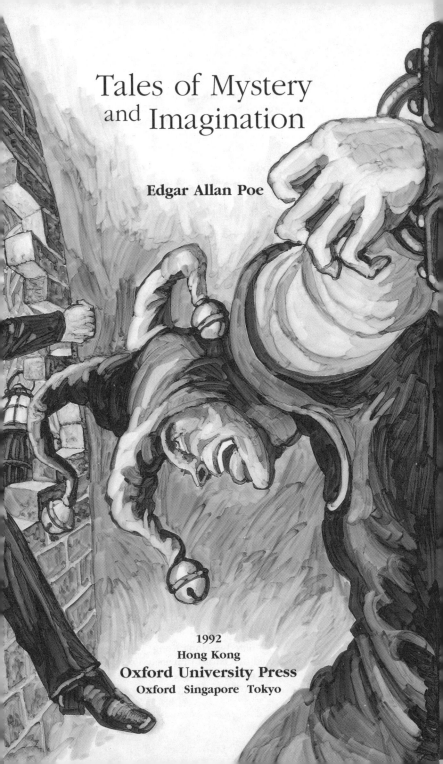

Tales of Mystery and Imagination

Edgar Allan Poe

1992
Hong Kong
Oxford University Press
Oxford Singapore Tokyo

Oxford University Press

Oxford   New York   Toronto   Madrid
Kuala Lumpur   Singapore   Hong Kong   Tokyo
Delhi   Bombay   Calcutta   Madras   Karachi
Nairobi   Dar es Salaam   Cape Town
Melbourne   Auckland

and associated companies in
Berlin   Ibadan

Illustrated by K.Y. Chan

Syllabus designer: David Foulds

Text processing and analysis by Luxfield Consultants Ltd.

ISBN 0 19 585463 2

Printed in Hong Kong
Published by Oxford University Press,
18/F Warwick House, Tong Chong Street,
Quarry Bay, Hong Kong

CONTENTS

CONTENTS

1

THE PIT AND THE PENDULUM

Cruel judges

I felt a terrible pain. It made me feel so sick that I nearly died. When they untied me at last, and I was allowed to sit up, I felt that my senses would leave me and that I would faint. I heard the judge say the word 'death'. That was the last thing I was sure I heard.

After that, the sound of the questioning voices seemed mixed and unclear, like a dim noise from far away. Yet, for a while, I saw the lips of the judges speaking to me. They appeared to me to be white, whiter than the piece of paper upon which I write these words, and cruelly thin. Then, when I saw all the horror surrounding me, I began to think how peaceful it must be in a grave. But while I was trying to think about this quiet end, rather than all the horrors and pain I must go through first, everything went silent and still, and all was black. I had fainted.

Very suddenly, I realized that I could hear the sound of my heart beating. Then, even more suddenly, all that had happened to me passed through my mind. I was so terrified by what I remembered that I did not want to recover from my faint. I could remember every detail of the trial, the faces of the judges, that I was to die by order of the court, and that at the end I had fainted. But I did not know how long ago all that had been.

So far, I had not opened my eyes. I could feel that I was lying on my back, and that I was not tied. I reached out my hand, and it fell heavily upon something damp and hard. I let it lie there for many minutes while I tried to imagine where I could be. I wanted to use my sight, but did not dare. I was so afraid of what I might find

around me. I especially feared that there might, indeed, be nothing to see. At last, with a wild beat of my heart, I quickly opened my eyes. My worst thoughts, then, were true. The blackness of everlasting night closed in around
5   me.

I felt that I could not breathe. I lay quietly and tried to control myself. I tried to make my brain work so that I could defeat my terror in that way. I knew that the court had ordered my death, and now that my mind was clearer,
10   I did not think that the trial had been very long ago. I knew definitely that I was not yet dead. I knew too, that people like me were usually burned to death. There had been a death by burning at the same time as my trial. Perhaps I had been put back in my prison cell to await a
15   similar end. Perhaps I would wait for many months. Then I realized that this was not probable. The people in the city demanded blood, and death.

Staring into the darkness

20   A fearful idea now suddenly sent the blood rushing to my heart, and I fainted again. When I recovered, I at once jumped to my feet, trembling all over. I pushed out my arms wildly above and around me in all directions. I felt nothing, but I was terrified to move a step in case I went
25   straight into a wall. I had the terrible thought in my mind that they might have buried me alive underground. The sweat collected on my forehead in big drops.

I stopped waving my hands around and stood there at last, still as a stone. Then I moved carefully forward, with
30   my arms stretched out in front of me. My eyes stared hard into the darkness, hoping to see some faint ray of light. I went forward for a number of steps, but all was blackness, and I could feel nothing. I began to breathe more easily. It seemed that at least I had not been buried
35   alive.

As I continued to step carefully forward, I remembered all the dreadful stories about the horrors that were to be found in this prison. People used to whisper in fear about what happened here. Perhaps I had been left to starve to death in this strange underground cell. Or perhaps something even more terrible was about to happen to me. Whatever it was that awaited me, I knew my judges well enough to feel sure that the result would be death. They never changed their decisions. I was only uncertain about how, and when, I would die.

Measuring my cell

At last my hands touched something. It was a stone wall, very smooth, damp and cold. I followed it around, walking carefully all the time. While I was doing this, however, I realized that I might pass the point where I had first touched the wall without knowing it. If that happened I would not know what kind of cell I was in, nor how big it was. I was especially confused because the wall seemed to be perfectly smooth, with no corners. I therefore looked for the knife that had been in my pocket, before my trial. It was gone, and I found to my surprise that my clothes had been replaced by a rough, dirty robe.

I had thought of forcing the knife into one of the gaps between the stones of the wall, to mark a place I would know I had passed before. My problem was easily solved, although at first, in my weakened state, I had thought it very difficult. I tore off a piece of cloth from the robe and placed it on the floor at the bottom of the wall. It would be in my path and I would certainly feel it as I completed my walk round the cell. At least, that is what I thought, but I had forgotten my own weakness, and I had no idea how big the cell in fact was.

The floor was damp and slippery. I walked on for some time, supporting myself against the wall. Then I found I was too weak to take another step forward. I slipped and fell to the ground. I was so tired that I could not get up again, and soon I fell asleep on that damp, cold floor.

5   When I woke up, I stretched out my arm, and to my surprise I found beside me a loaf of bread and a cup of water. I was too tired and weak to wonder how these things had got there, but only ate and drank eagerly. Soon afterwards, I restarted the tour of my prison, and at last I

10   found the piece of cloth I had left lying against the wall.

Up to the period when I fell, I had counted fifty-two steps. When I restarted, I counted forty-eight more before I got back to the cloth. There were altogether, then, one hundred steps. Taking two steps to be a yard, I thought

15   my cell must be about fifty yards all round. While I walked, though, I had found odd angles in the wall, and so I could not guess the shape of the cell.

I had no reason or plan for what I was doing — and certainly no hope — but curiosity made me continue.

20   Leaving the support of the wall, I decided that I would cross the centre of the cell to the other side. At first I went very carefully, for the floor, although it seemed solid, was very slippery. Finally, however, I became braver, and walked out firmly, trying to cross in as straight a line as

25   possible. I had advanced about ten or twelve steps in this way, when the end of my torn robe became caught between my legs. I stepped on it, and fell violently on my face.

The deep, dark pit

In the confusion caused by my fall, I did not immediately

30   realize a very frightening thing, which, a few seconds later, and while I still lay face down on the floor, caught my attention. It was this — my chin rested on the floor of the prison, but my lips and the upper part of my head, although they were bent lower than my chin, touched

nothing. I reached out my arm, and shook with terror when I realized that I had fallen on the very edge of a large circular hole in the floor. Of course, I had no way of telling at that moment how big, or how deep it was. I broke off a piece of stone from the edge of the hole, and let it fall into the blackness in front of me. For many seconds I listened for its landing. Then, at last, there was the sound of a sudden splash into water. At the same moment, I heard something like the quick opening and closing of a door above me. A faint ray of light flashed suddenly through the darkness, and equally suddenly faded away.

Then I realized the death that they had prepared for me. I smiled to myself with relief at the accident which had caused me to escape from such a death. Another step before my fall, and the world would never have seen me again. Shaking all over, I crawled back to the wall. I decided that it would be better to die there than to risk the terror of the pit.

Realizing the truth

I was so terrified and upset that I stayed awake for many long hours, but at last I slept. When I woke, I found by my side, as before, a loaf of bread and a cup of water. I was very thirsty, and drank all the water at once. There must have been something in it, for as soon as I put the

cup down, I fell asleep. It was a deep sleep, like the sleep
of death. I do not know how long it lasted, but when I
opened my eyes again, the objects around me could be
seen. I could see how large the cell was and what it
looked like.

I had been greatly mistaken in its size. The length
around its walls could not have been more than twenty-
five yards. For some minutes this fact worried me more
than anything else, though it may sound strange. For it
was so unimportant, when I knew that death, in some
form, would soon come to me. Why should the size of
my cell worry me? But it did trouble me, and I was
determined to discover why I had made an error in my
earlier measurements.

At last I realized the truth. In my first attempt to go
round the cell, I had counted fifty-two steps, up to the
period when I fell. I must then have been within a step
or two of the piece of cloth. In fact, I had nearly gone
round the whole cell. I then slept, and when I woke, I
must have gone back the way I had come, not forward.
Therefore I had made myself think that the cell was nearly
twice the size that it actually was. My confusion of mind
must have prevented me from noticing that I had begun
my tour with the wall on my left, and ended it with the
wall on my right.

I had not been right, also, about the shape of the cell.
In feeling my way, I had found many angles, and thus
thought that the cell was a very odd shape. It proves the
effect of total darkness on a man who is both mentally
and physically tired. The angles, which seemed to form a
major part in the shape of the cell, were simply a few
uneven stones that appeared at odd places. The general
shape of the cell was square. I now noticed the floor, too,
which was of stone. In the centre was the circular pit that
I had so nearly fallen into.

I saw all this with difficulty. My physical position had
been greatly changed while I had been sleeping. I now

lay upon my back, stretched out fully, on a low wooden board. I was tied to this board by a long, strong strap that went round and round my body, leaving free only my head, and my left arm. With effort I could reach the food that lay in a dish by my side on the floor. I saw, to my horror, that the cup of water had been removed. I was terribly thirsty, but there was no water to make me feel better.

A clock with a pendulum

Looking upwards, I stared at the ceiling of my prison. It was about thirty or forty feet high. What especially caught my attention was a clock, supported on the great bars of wood that held up the ceiling, with a huge pendulum hanging from it. While I looked up at it (for it was directly above me), I thought that I could see the pendulum moving. I soon realized that I was right. It was moving slowly backwards and forwards. I watched it for some minutes, afraid but also curious. What could this mean? At last I became tired of the dull movement of the pendulum, and turned to look at the walls again.

A slight noise attracted my attention. I looked at the floor, and saw several enormous rats crossing it. They had come up from the pit, which lay just within view to my right. Even then, as I looked, many more rats came up over the edge. They came quickly, and had hungry eyes. They must have been attracted by the smell of the food beside me. It took all my energy and attention to keep them away from the food in the dish.

Long hours of horror

It could have been half an hour, perhaps even an hour, before I again looked up to the clock. What I saw then terrified and amazed me. The length of swing of the pendulum from side to side had increased by nearly a

yard, and the pendulum now moved back and forth much
faster. But what disturbed me most was that I was certain
it was lower than it had been. I now saw, with horror,
that at the bottom of the pendulum there was a piece of
5   steel in the shape of a quarter moon. It was about a foot
in length from curved point to curved point. The points
were facing upwards, and the bottom, outer edge was
obviously as sharp as a butcher's knife. It looked heavy
and dangerous, and was full of dreadful terror for me. The
10   pendulum hissed wickedly as it swung through the air.

Now I knew the kind of death that my judges had
arranged for me. They had given up the idea of the pit
once I had discovered it. They realized that now I would
not fall down into it without being pushed, and they did
15   not intend to do that. So, they had decided on the
pendulum for me instead!

How can I tell of the long, long hours of horror, during
which I counted the rushing swings of that piece of
steel! It came down inch by inch. Perhaps
20   many days passed before the pendulum
swept so closely that I could feel the
air blowing over me with each
steady movement. I swear
I could smell the sharp
25   steel as it swept past.

I prayed for a quick descent of the pendulum. I struggled like a madman, and tried to force myself upward against its knife-like blade. And then I fell suddenly calm, and lay smiling up at the pendulum that would kill me. I was waiting for it as eagerly as a child waits to be given a toy.

Then I fainted again. It was only for a short time, I think, for when I recovered I could see little change in the descent of the pendulum. I felt sick and weak, but in spite of my pain and terror, I was hungry. With a painful effort, I stretched out my left arm as far as I could, and ate some of the food that had not been taken by the rats.

The pendulum comes closer

The pendulum was swinging across my body at right angles to my length. I could see that the bottom edge of the pendulum was set to cross the area of my heart. It would cut through the cloth of my robe. It would return and repeat its work, again and again. Yet in spite of its very wide swing (some thirty feet or more) and the hissing movement of its descent, the pendulum would take several minutes to cut through my robe, because it was descending so slowly.

It crept steadily down. It moved to the right, to the left, far and wide. With a hiss like the devil himself, it moved down slowly towards my heart, as cruel as a tiger! Down — always, always down! It came to within three inches of my chest! I struggled violently to free my left arm. This was free only from the elbow to the hand. With a great effort I could reach the food on my left and put it to my mouth, and that was all. If I had been able to loosen the strap, which held my body above the elbow, I am sure I would have tried to seize the pendulum and stop its movement. It would have been easier to stop a mad bull!

It was still coming down! I struggled each time the pendulum crossed above my body. I shrank back each time it swung. My eyes followed its outward and upward movements with the eagerness of complete despair. My eyes closed each time the terrible thing passed over me. Death would have been a welcome relief.

5   **Faint hopes**

I saw that it would not be much longer before the steel would start to cut my robe. When I realized this, I became calm. For the first time in many hours, or perhaps days, I began to think carefully. I thought about the strap that
10 tied me down. It was most unusual, being of one long piece only. The first cut by the pendulum on the strap would mean that I might be able to pull the whole thing away from my body, with my left hand. But how frightening would be the closeness of the cutting steel!
15 The slightest mistake would end in death. And it was likely, too, that the people who had thought of this means of death had also thought of this very problem! It seemed unlikely, therefore, that the strap crossed my chest in the path of the pendulum.
20   I lifted my head as far as I could, to try to look at my chest. I was terrified that I would find my last, faint hope destroyed. At last I could see. The strap was tied closely round my arms, legs and body in all directions — except where the destroying pendulum would cut me.
25   I had hardly dropped my head back to its original position when I had a new thought of hope. I started at once, with the nervous energy of despair, to try to make it work.

For many hours, hundreds of rats had been crawling
30 all around me. They were wild, bold, hungry. Their red eyes looked at me as if they were only waiting for my death so that they could attack me. 'What dreadful food,' I wondered to myself, 'have they been eating in that pit?'

Although I had tried to stop them, they had eaten nearly
35 everything in the dish. I waved my hand above it

occasionally to chase them away, but at last the regular movement of my hand had made that useless. The rats no longer feared me, and frequently bit my fingers. Now, however, I wanted them to eat. I made my fingers sticky with what was left of the food, and then rubbed them on the strap, everywhere I could touch it. Soon the strap began to smell of food. Then I lay as still as possible.

The strap is loosened

At first, the hungry rats were frightened because the regular movement of my hand had stopped. They stayed away, and many went back into the pit. But this was only for a moment. Seeing that I remained without movement, one or two of the bravest leapt onto the piece of wood that I lay on, and smelt at the strap. This seemed to be a signal for a general rush. They leapt in hundreds onto my body. The regular movement of the pendulum did not seem to disturb them at all. Avoiding its swings, they were busy chewing at the strap. They crawled all over me, over my neck and face. Their noses and feet touched my mouth. I could hardly breathe because of them. Feelings for which the world has no name rose inside me, and my heart grew cold with horror. But I felt that the struggle would be over in a minute. I could clearly feel the strap loosening. I knew that it must already be broken in more than one place.

At last I was free. The strap hung from my body, chewed through in many places by the hungry rats. But the pendulum had already swung across my chest. It had split the cloth of my robe. Twice again it swung, and a sharp sense of pain went through every part of my body. But the moment of escape had arrived. At a wave of my hand, the rats, which had helped me, hurried away. Moving steadily and slowly sideways, I slid off the wooden board beyond the reach of the deadly pendulum. For the moment, at least, I was free.

No escape

Free! But I was still in the power of my judges! I had
hardly fallen from that wooden bed of horror onto the
stone floor of the prison, when the movement of the
5   horrible machine stopped. I saw it being drawn up, by
some unknown force, through the ceiling. My every move
must have been watched. Free! I had only escaped one
form of death to find that I must surely face another,
probably even more horrible.

10   Nervously I looked around at the walls of my prison.
Something unusual had taken place in the cell. Some
change which, at first, I could not see. While I was trying
to work out what it was, I noticed for the first time where
the light came from. It came from a crack, about half an
15   inch wide, which went completely round the cell at the
bottom of the walls. The walls were completely separated
from the floor. I tried to look through the crack, but of
course I could not see anything.

Immediately, I understood the mystery of the change
20   in the cell. The cell was much brighter, and it was the
kind of light given out by a fire!

As I watched, smoke began to come up through the
crack around the walls. A terrible smell entered the cell.
I could hardly breathe! There could be no doubt about
25   what my judges intended now! Among the thoughts of the
hot, burning death I was about to suffer, the idea of the
coolness of the pit came to me like a welcome escape. I
rushed to its deadly edge. I stared down into its depths.
Yet for a wild moment, I refused to realize what I was
30   really looking at — death in the pit. But at last my senses
returned and I ran screaming from its edge. I buried my
face in my hands. Was there to be no escape from these
horrors?

The heat rapidly increased, and once again I looked
35   up. There had been a second change in the cell. As
before, at first I could not understand exactly what the

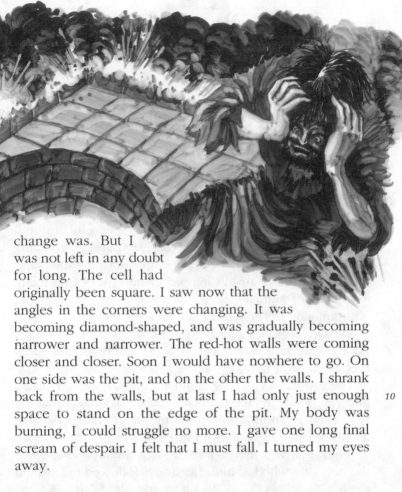

change was. But I
was not left in any doubt
for long. The cell had
originally been square. I saw now that the
angles in the corners were changing. It was
becoming diamond-shaped, and was gradually becoming
narrower and narrower. The red-hot walls were coming
closer and closer. Soon I would have nowhere to go. On
one side was the pit, and on the other the walls. I shrank
back from the walls, but at last I had only just enough   10
space to stand on the edge of the pit. My body was
burning, I could struggle no more. I gave one long final
scream of despair. I felt that I must fall. I turned my eyes
away.

Rescue   15

Suddenly I heard loud shouts coming from all around me!
There was the noise of shooting and men fighting! The
horrible walls rushed back to their normal position. An
arm stretched out and caught me as I fell, fainting, towards
the pit. It was the arm of my friend, the General. His brave 20
soldiers had entered this most dreadful of prisons, and my
cruel judges were now in the hands of their enemies.

2

THE BLACK CAT

A love of animals

I do not expect you to believe the wild story I am about to write. I would be mad to expect you to believe it. Even my reason tells me it is difficult to believe. Yet I am not
5 mad, and I am not dreaming. But in order to die peacefully, I must tell my story.

When I was a child, I was very kind, peaceful, and full of love. I was very fond of animals. My parents, knowing this, let me have many pets. I spent most of my time with
10 my pets, and was always happiest when I was with them. This love of animals stayed with me as an adult. Being with animals still remained my greatest pleasure.

I married young, and my wife shared my love for animals. We had many pets — birds, goldfish, a fine dog,
15 rabbits, a small monkey, and a cat.

The cat was a large, beautiful animal, completely black, and very wise. In fact, the black cat was so clever that my wife used to laugh and remind me of the old belief that all black cats are witches in disguise.

20 Pluto, that was the cat's name, was my favourite. I was the only one who fed him. He always followed me around the house. It was even difficult to stop him from following me into the street.

My friendship with this cat lasted happily for several
25 years. Then a weakness of mine began to alter my whole character. I started drinking. Day by day, I became more and more unpleasant. I took no notice of anybody else's feelings. I started to swear at my wife. In the end, I even started to hit her. My pets, of course, also suffered from
30 my bad temper. I not only took no notice of them, but I

also treated
them very badly. The
rabbits, the monkey and even
the dog suffered through no fault of
their own. Pluto, though, I still loved   5
enough to leave alone. But my drinking grew worse and
worse until even Pluto began to suffer from my
uncontrollable temper.

I do something terrible

One night, I came home very drunk. I had been drinking   10
all day. I was in a very bad temper. For some reason, Pluto
made me angry. I thought he was trying to avoid me. I
seized him. He must have been afraid of my violence, and
he struggled to get away. In doing so, he scratched my
hand. I knew that he had not meant to harm me, but I   15
no longer had any control over myself. I was terribly
angry. I was determined to punish that poor innocent cat.
In a rage I took a small knife out of my pocket. I held
the cat by the throat, and cut out one of its eyes!

The next morning, when I woke up, I remembered my terrible crime. For a short time I was sorry for what I had done, but the feeling did not last long. I was soon drinking again. This time I drank to forget what I had done.

5   The cat slowly recovered. There was a terrible wound where his eye had been, but after a while he no longer seemed to suffer pain from it. He went about the house as usual. Every time he heard me coming, however, he would run away in fear. At first I was upset by his

10 behaviour, because I remembered how much Pluto had once loved me. But soon his obvious dislike for me began to make me angry. In the end, I could not bear it. One morning I caught poor Pluto, and then I put a rope around his neck, and hanged him from the branch of a tree. I

15 hanged that poor creature until he was dead.

My house burns down

That night, I was woken from my sleep by the loud voices of people shouting that the house was burning. My wife and I and the servant only just escaped in time. The whole

20 house was destroyed. There was nothing left.

    I do not know if there was any real connection between the terrible thing I had done to Pluto and the burning of my house, but other strange things began to happen.

    The day after the fire, I went back to look at the ruins

25 of my home. All of the walls, except one, had fallen down. Strangely enough, it was my bedroom wall. When I got there, a large crowd was standing round this one remaining wall. I could hear people saying, 'Strange!', 'Odd!'. I wondered what it was they were looking at. I

30 went up to the wall, and saw, as though drawn on to the wall, the shape of a huge cat. It was quite clear. There seemed to be a rope around the animal's neck.

    When I saw this, I was terrified and amazed. For months, even though I had moved to a new house, I could

not forget that strange sight. I even began to feel sorry
that I had killed Pluto. I began to search for another cat
like him, to take his place.

A new pet

One night, when I was sitting in a restaurant, I saw a black   5
object on the floor. I had been drinking a lot, and did not
at first realize what I was looking at. Then I realized, it
was a black cat. It was very big, just as big as Pluto, and
looked almost exactly the same. There was only one
difference. Pluto had been completely black. This cat had   10
a small patch of white fur on his chest.

I got up and went to the cat. When I touched him, he
was very friendly and seemed to like me stroking him. I
was sure that this was the animal I wanted to have instead
of Pluto. I asked the owner of the place if I could buy   15
the cat from him. He said the cat did not belong to him,
and he had never seen it before.

I continued to stroke the cat, and, when I decided to
go home, the animal started to follow me. It followed me
all the way. I took it into my house, and it immediately   20
became a great favourite with my wife.

As for myself, I soon began to dislike my new pet. I
don't know why, for the cat obviously loved me. I began
to hate that animal. At first I tried to avoid seeing it. I was
ashamed of what I had done to Pluto, and I did not want   25
to do the same thing to this cat.

There was one thing that added to my dislike of the
animal. The morning after I brought it home, I saw that
it had only one eye.

The more I grew to hate this cat, the more it seemed   30
to love me. It followed me everywhere. If I sat down, it
would sit underneath my chair, or jump up onto me. If I
got up to walk, it would get between my feet and nearly
trip me over. It would climb up my clothes until it reached
my arms, and then I would have to hold it.   35

The cat began to terrify me. I don't know why, for it was only a cat. I became more and more bad-tempered, and more difficult to live with. My poor uncomplaining wife suffered so much.

⁵   ### I murder my wife

One day, my wife and I both went down to the cellar, for some reason. The cat followed us. It got between my feet and nearly made me trip down the steep stairs. I was carrying an axe in my hand, and I was so angry
¹⁰ with the cat that I raised the axe with the intention of hitting the poor animal. My wife tried to stop me from doing such a terrible thing.

My rage at once directed itself at her instead of the cat. Without thinking, I freed myself from her hold and buried the axe in her head. She fell dead at my feet, without making a sound.

I had murdered my wife. Coolly, and without any feelings of sorrow for what I had done, I decided that I must hide the body. I knew that I could not remove it from the house without being seen by the neighbours. Many ideas passed through my mind. At one period, I thought of cutting the body into pieces and burning it. After that I thought of digging a grave in the floor of the cellar and burying the body there. Then I thought of packing the body in a box, and getting someone to take the box from the house. Finally, I decided on what I thought was the best idea. I decided to bury my wife inside one of the cellar walls.

The cellar was a very good place to do this terrible thing. The walls were quite soft because of the damp air. And, most important of all, in one place, a chimney had been covered over and the wall made smooth and flat, so as to look just like the other walls in the cellar. I was sure that I could easily remove the bricks from in front of the old fireplace, put my wife inside, and then build the wall again so that no one could tell what had happened.

I did exactly as I had planned. When I had finished, I felt satisfied that no one would know what I had done. The wall looked exactly the same as before, and no different to any of the other walls.

Once I had done that, I decided to look for the animal that had caused this crime to happen. I had decided to kill it too, but I couldn't find it anywhere. Three days passed, and still the cat did not reappear.

It was a lovely feeling to think that the cat had gone. The guilt of my wife's murder did not bother me at all. Some neighbours asked me where she was, but I easily made up some story that satisfied their curiosity. Or so I thought.

The voice from behind the wall

On the fourth day after the death of my wife, I had an unexpected visit from the police, who searched the house. However, I was certain that they would never find my hiding place. I was not at all worried. The police made me go with them as they searched. They looked in the cellar four times, but they found nothing. My heart beat quite calmly. I behaved as if I was completely innocent. At last, the police seemed satisfied with their search and were about to leave. I was so pleased with myself that I had to say something

'Gentlemen,' I said at last, as the police were about to go up the cellar steps, 'I am delighted that your suspicions are now at rest. By the way, gentlemen, this is a well-built house.' For some reason I had a stupid desire to boast, and hardly knew what I was saying. 'It is very strongly built, look at these walls.' And to show how strong the walls were, I lifted the stick I was holding, and beat the wall behind which I had buried my wife.

As soon as I had done that, a voice cried out from behind the wall! It sounded like the crying of a child.

I was horrified, and fell back against the opposite wall. The police stood completely still on the stairs, with looks of horror and amazement on their faces. One moment they were quite still, the next they were tearing down the wall. The body of my wife became visible almost immediately. And sitting in front of her dead body was that horrible one-eyed cat. It was the cat that had caused me to murder my wife, and the cat that had now made the murder known to the police. That cat would cause me to be hanged as I had hanged Pluto!

When I had buried my wife in the wall, the cat had somehow got into that awful grave with her!

3

THE MURDERS IN THE STREET
OF DEATH

An ability to observe details

During the spring and summer of 1802, I lived in Paris. One of the people I met, and came to know well there, was a man named Mr Dupin. This young gentleman came from an excellent and important family, but, because of a number of unfortunate events, he had become rather poor. Mr Dupin could no longer walk about the town proudly. He was in some ways a broken man. In fact, it was only because of the kindness of some people who had lent him money, that he had any money left at all. But he used this money carefully, and he was at least able to live simply. He allowed himself only one pleasure, books. He loved books, and in Paris these are easily obtained.

Our first meeting was in a small, little-used library, where we were both looking for the same book. It was a rare book, and as we were both interested in it, we started up a conversation. Soon after that we met quite frequently.

I was deeply interested in his family history. He seemed very pleased to tell me about himself and his family. I was astonished, too, at how much he had read. Above all, I liked the freshness of his imagination. I felt that the friendship of such a man would be a treasure beyond price to me. At last, we arranged that we should share a home together during my stay in the city. As I had more money than he did, it was agreed that I would rent a suitable house for both of us. I found exactly what we wanted in the area known as St Germain. The house was large and old. People said there were ghosts in it, but the ghosts did not worry us at all. We loved our strange home.

If the world had known how we lived, it would have thought we were mad, although probably harmless. Our peace was perfect. We allowed no visitors. Indeed, I did not tell any of my former friends where I had moved to, and it had been many years since Dupin had met any of *his* former friends in Paris.

5   One of the strange things about my new friend was that he loved the night time, and I agreed with his wishes to try to keep the darkness with us all the time. At the first light of dawn, each morning, we closed all the shutters in our old building, and lit candles, which gave only the
10   weakest light. With the help of these, we then spent the time reading, writing, or talking, until we were warned by the striking of the clock of the coming of true darkness. Then we went out into the streets, arm in arm, continuing to talk about the subjects of the day. Or we walked far
15   and wide until a late hour, looking for our pleasures among the wild lights and shadows of the busy city, pleasures that can only be found from quietly observing such scenes.

At such times, I could not help admiring the ability
20   Dupin had for observing the smallest details. He often noticed things which seemed to have no connection or importance, but he gained knowledge and information from them that most people would never dream of. He seemed to take an eager delight in using this ability, and
25   did not hesitate to tell me of the pleasure he obtained from it. He boasted to me, with a low laugh, that, to him, most men wore windows in their hearts. He used to prove this by telling me something about myself that I had certainly never told him before, but which he managed to
30   know by putting together a large number of facts which did not seem to be connected.

A horrifying and amazing crime

Not long after I had noticed this peculiar ability of Dupin's, we were looking through an evening newspaper and read
35   the following paragraphs:

EXTRAORDINARY MURDERS

This morning, at about three o'clock, the inhabitants of La Rochelle, in Paris, were woken from their sleep by terrible screams, coming from the fourth floor of a house in that area. The house was 5 *owned by a Mrs Spain, and her daughter, Camelia Spain. After some delay, two policemen entered the house by breaking open the door. They were followed by about ten curious neighbours.*

By this time, the screaming had stopped, but as 10 *the people rushed up the stairs, they seemed to hear two or more rough voices arguing. The voices came from the upper part of the house. As the people reached the second floor, these sounds also stopped, and everything was perfectly quiet.* 15

The house was searched. The policemen arrived at a large back room on the fourth floor and forced open the door, which was locked from the inside. They and the neighbours saw a sight which horrified and amazed them all. 20

The room was in wild disorder. The furniture was broken and thrown about in all directions. There was only one bed, and from this, all the covers had been removed, and thrown into the middle of the floor. On a chair lay a sharp razor, covered with 25 *blood. In front of the fire were two or three long, thick bunches of grey human hair, which seemed to have been pulled out by the roots. Personal articles including a ring, three large silver spoons, and two bags, containing nearly 4,000 francs in* 30 *gold, were lying on the floor. The drawers of a dressing table were open, and had been searched, although many articles were still untouched. A small iron strong-box was discovered under the bed. It was open, with a key still in the lock. The* 35 *only contents were a few old letters, and other papers of no importance.*

*No one could see
Mrs Spain in the room.
Because there were unusually*

5   *large amounts of dirt and ashes in the fireplace,
which seemed to have fallen from the chimney, a
search was made of the chimney itself. Then, the
dead body of the daughter, head down, was dragged
from it. The body was quite warm. When the body
was examined, many cuts and bruises were*

10 *discovered, no doubt caused by the violence with
which it had been forced up the chimney. There were
severe scratches on the face, and, around the neck,
some deep blue bruises left by finger marks. It looked
as if the dead girl had been strangled.*

15 *After the whole house had been completely
searched, without finding the mother, the police and
the rest of the party made their way into a small
yard at the back of the building. There they found
the body of Mrs Spain. Her throat had been so badly*

20 *cut that, when she was lifted up, her head fell off.*

*We believe that at present the police are quite
unable to explain this horrible crime.*

Witnesses

The next day's paper had some more news on the subject:

THE MURDERS IN THE STREET OF DEATH

Many people have been questioned about this most extraordinary and frightening mystery, but not a single clue has been found. We give below all the evidence the police have obtained from a number of witnesses.

The first witness, a washerwoman, says that she had known both of the dead women for three years, having washed clothes for them during that period. The old lady and her daughter seemed to be very friendly towards each other. They paid her well for the washing she did for them. She could not say where their money came from, nor in what style they lived. She believed that Mrs Spain told fortunes for a living. People said that Mrs Spain had quite a lot of money. The witness never met any visitors in the house when she called for the clothes or returned them. She was certain that they did not employ a servant. There appeared to be no furniture in any part of the building, except on the fourth floor.

The second witness, the owner of a tobacco shop, says that he sold small quantities of tobacco and other articles to Mrs Spain for nearly four years. He was born in the neighbourhood, and has always lived there. Mrs Spain and her daughter had lived in the house where their bodies were found for more than six years. Before that, she had rented it to a jeweller. She had become displeased with the way he was looking after the house and had moved in herself. The witness saw the daughter some five or six times during the six years. They lived very quietly, and people thought they had money. He had heard it said that Mrs Spain told fortunes, but he did not

5

10

15

20

25

30

35

believe it. He had never seen anyone enter through the front door, except the old lady and her daughter, a tradesman once or twice, and a doctor some eight or ten times.

5   *Many other people, neighbours, gave similar evidence. No one spoke of frequent visitors to the house. The shutters of the front windows were seldom opened, and at the back of the house, they were always closed, except those of the large back room on the*
10   *fourth floor. The house is well built, and not very old.*

The third witness, a policeman, says that he was called to the house at about three o'clock in the morning, and found a large number of people at the front door, trying to get in. He forced the door
15   *open, in the end, with an iron bar. The screams continued until the door was opened, and then they suddenly stopped. They seemed to be the screams of some person (or persons) in great pain. They were loud and long, not short and quick.*

20   *The witness led the way upstairs. When he reached the first floor, he heard two loud voices arguing — one fairly deep and the other much higher, a very strange voice. He could understand some words of the former, which was that of a Frenchman. He was*
25   *sure that it was not a woman's voice. He heard the words 'Heavens' and 'dreadful'. The high voice was that of a foreigner, speaking quickly and unevenly. He could not be sure whether it was the voice of a man or of a woman. He could not understand what*
30   *was said, but he believed the language to be Spanish. The room and the bodies were described by this witness as we described them yesterday.*

The fourth witness, a neighbour and a silver merchant, says that he was one of the people who
35   *first entered the house. He says much the same as the policeman. As soon as they went inside the house, they closed the door to keep out the crowd, which*

*had collected very fast even though it was very late.
The high voice, this witness thinks, was that of an
Italian. He was certain that it was not French. He
could not be sure that it was a man's voice. It might
have been a woman's. He does not understand the* 5
*Italian language, so he could not make out any
words, but he was convinced by the rise and fall of
the voice that the speaker was an Italian. He knew
Mrs Spain and her daughter. He had talked to both
of them often. He was sure that the high voice was* 10
not that of either of the dead women.

*The fifth witness is a Dutch restaurant owner. He
cannot speak French, so he was questioned by an
interpreter who knew both French and Dutch. The
witness comes from Amsterdam. He was passing the* 15
*house when he heard the screams. They lasted
several minutes — probably ten. They were long and
loud — very awful and upsetting. He was one of
those who entered the building. He agreed with all
the other evidence except on one point. He was sure* 20
*that the high voice was that of a man — of a
Frenchman. He could not make out the words
spoken. They were loud and quick. He thought they
were spoken in fear as well as in anger. The voice
was harsh, rather than high.* 25

*The sixth witness is a bank manager. Mrs Spain
had some property, and had opened an account with
his bank eight years ago. She often paid in cash, in
small amounts. She had asked to take out nothing
until the third day before her death, when she asked* 30
*for 4,000 francs. This amount was paid in gold, and
a clerk was sent to her house with the money.*

*The seventh witness, a clerk at the same bank, says
that on the day of the murders, at about noon, he
went with Mrs Spain to her house, with the 4,000* 35
*francs in two bags. When the door opened, Miss
Spain appeared and took one of the bags from his*

hands, while the old lady took the other. He then bowed and left. He did not see anyone in the street at the time. It is a small and very quiet street.

The eighth witness, a tailor, says that he was one of the people who entered the house. He is an Englishman. He has lived in Paris for two years. He was one of the first to go upstairs and he heard the voices arguing. The deep voice was that of a Frenchman. He could make out several words, but he cannot remember all of them now. He heard quite clearly 'Heavens' and 'My God'. Then there was a sound at that moment as if several people were struggling. The high voice was very loud, louder than the deep one. He is sure that the voice was not the voice of an Englishman. It appeared to be that of a German. It might have been a woman's voice. He does not understand German.

Four of these witnesses, being called back by the police, said that the door of the room, in which the body of Miss Spain was found, was locked from the inside when the party reached it. Everything was perfectly silent. There were no noises of any kind. When the door was forced open, the witnesses could not see anyone in the room. The front and back windows were closed and firmly shut from the inside. The door to a small room in the front of the house, on the fourth floor, at the head of the hall,

*was open slightly. This room was crowded with old
beds, boxes, and so on, which were carefully
removed and searched. There was not an inch of
any part of the house that was not carefully
searched. Even the chimneys were searched.*   5

*The witnesses were asked how much time passed
between the moment they heard the voices arguing
and the moment the door of the room where Miss
Spain's body was found was broken open. Some said
it was as short as three minutes, some as long as*   10
five. The door was opened with some difficulty.

*The ninth witness is Spanish. He was one of the
people who entered the house, but he did not go
upstairs. He says he was too nervous. He heard the
voices arguing. The deep voice was that of a*   15
*Frenchman. He could not tell what was said. He is
sure that the high voice was that of an Englishman.
He does not understand the English language, but
judges by the sounds.*

Several witnesses, when asked further questions,   20
*said that there was definitely no way out of the
building except through the front door. The chimneys
were too small to climb up; the body of Miss Spain
fitted so closely into the chimney that it took four or
five men using their combined strength to pull her*   25
*down. All the windows in the house were closed, and
locked from the inside.*

*The official doctor's report, after giving all the
medical details of the condition of the two women's
bodies, concludes that it is not possible to say exactly*   30
*how the injuries were caused. A heavy weapon of
some kind would have produced such results, if used
by someone who was unusually strong. The head of
the mother, when seen by the doctor, had been
completely separated from the body. The throat had*   35
*obviously been cut with something very sharp,
probably with the razor.*

Nothing further of importance was discovered,
although several other persons were questioned.
Never before, in Paris, has there been a murder
so mysterious, and so odd in all its details. There
5   *does not seem to be even one small clue for the police*
to follow.

The evening paper stated that great activity and
excitement still continued in the district. The house had
been carefully searched, and the witnesses questioned
10   again, but with no success. A late newspaper, however,
mentioned that the bank clerk had been arrested and was
being held by the police, but they had no evidence against
him.

Dupin wants to solve the mystery

15   Dupin seemed very interested in this business, and after
we heard the news that the clerk had been arrested, he
asked what I thought about the murders.

I could only agree with the rest of Paris in considering
them an impossible mystery. I could think of no way of
20   finding the murderer.

'We cannot discover the answer,' said Dupin, 'from what
has been written in this paper. We must examine
everything for ourselves before we form an opinion about
what really happened. It will be quite amusing.' I thought
25   this an odd way to look at the murders, but said nothing.
'Besides,' Dupin continued, 'I believe I know that bank
clerk. He helped me once, and I am very grateful for what
he did. I would like to help him. We will go and see the
house with our own eyes. I know the Chief of Police, and
30   it will be easy to get the necessary permission.'

The permission was obtained, and we went at once to
the street that had now become known as the Street of
Death. It was late in the afternoon when we reached it.
The house was easily found, for there were still many

people looking up at its closed shutters. It was an ordinary
Parisian house. Before we went inside, Dupin looked
around the whole neighbourhood very carefully, as well
as examining the outside of the house. I could not see
the purpose of such a detailed examination at all.   5

A policeman then let us into the house and went with
us everywhere inside. I saw nothing more than what had
already been described in the newspaper. Dupin looked
at everything. We even had to go and look at the bodies
of the victims. We then went into the other rooms, and   10
into the yard. The examination occupied us till dark, when
we left. On our way home, my companion went into the
office of one of the daily papers.

'Did you see anything peculiar?'

My strange friend now refused to talk about the murders   15
until about noon the next day. He then asked me,
suddenly, if I had observed anything peculiar at the scene
of the crime.

There was something about the way that he said the
word 'peculiar' which made me feel uneasy, without   20
knowing why.

'No, nothing peculiar,' I said. 'Nothing more than the
details we both read in the newspaper.'

'The paper,' he replied, 'has not really understood, I
fear, the unusual horror of the thing. But forget the   25
opinions of the paper. It appears to me that people think
this mystery cannot be solved, but I think, for the same
reason, that it should be easy to solve. The police are
confused by the lack of a good reason for the murders,
and by the special horror of the murders. They are   30
puzzled, too, by the fact that two voices were heard
arguing but no one was discovered alive upstairs. The only
person they found there was Miss Spain, who was clearly
quite dead. There was no way of getting out of the house
without being seen by the people coming up the stairs.   35

The terrible disorder of the room, the body of Miss Spain pushed up the chimney, the frightful condition of the body of Mrs Spain — all these facts have completely fooled the police as to why and who killed those two unfortunate
5   women. In an inquiry like this, we should not just ask "What has happened?" but "What has happened that has never happened before?" '

I stared at Dupin in silent amazement.

'I am now waiting,' he continued, looking towards the
10   door of our house, 'for a person who, although perhaps not the murderer of these women, must have been involved in their deaths. It is true that he may not come, but he probably will. When he does, it will be necessary to keep him here. Here are two guns. We both know how
15   to use them if necessary.'

I took the gun that he gave me, hardly realizing what I did, or believing what I heard. Dupin went on,
20   as if he was talking to himself.

'The evidence proved,' he said, 'that the voices heard by the
25   people on the stairs, were not the voices of the women. This means that the old woman could not have first
30   destroyed the daughter, and afterwards killed herself. I mention this point so that we do not waste time thinking about things that will lead us nowhere. Mrs Spain would not
35   have been strong enough to push her daughter's body up the chimney, and the nature of the wounds upon her own body means that it would have been impossible to have

killed herself in such a way. So someone else committed
the murders. The voice of this someone else was heard
arguing. Let me now discuss what was peculiar about the
evidence concerning these voices. Did you notice
anything peculiar about it?'   5

The high voice

I said that, while all the witnesses agreed that the deep
voice was that of a Frenchman, there was much
disagreement about the high, or as one person called it,
the harsh voice.   10
   'That was the evidence itself,' said Dupin, 'but it was
not the strangeness of the evidence. You have observed
nothing important. Yet there was something to be
observed. The witnesses, as you say, agreed about the
deep voice. But when talking about the high voice, an   15
Englishman, a Spaniard, a Dutchman, and a Frenchman
all tried to describe it, and each one thought they had
heard the voice of a foreigner. Each is sure that it was not
the voice of one of his own countrymen. Each thinks of
it as a language that he does not know. The Frenchman   20
thinks it is the voice of a Spaniard, but he does not know
Spanish. The Dutchman insists it was that of a Frenchman,
but we know that he does not understand French because
he had to be questioned by an interpreter. The Englishman
thinks it is the voice of a German, but does not understand 25
German. Now, how unusual that voice must have been,
to have caused such odd evidence! So many different
Europeans could not recognize anything familiar in the
tones! You will say that it might have been the voice of
an Asian or of an African. Neither Asians nor Africans are   30
in Paris in great numbers. I shall not deny that it is
possible, but I will now call your attention to three points.
The voice is called by one witness "harsh rather than
high." Two others called it "quick and uneven." No
witnesses mentioned recognizing any words.   35

'I do not know,' continued Dupin, 'what you may have decided so far from what I have been saying, but you must agree that I have made a little progress. Please remember that.'

How did the murderer escape?

'Let us now pretend that we are back at the house where the women were found dead. What shall we first look for? The means of escape used by the murderer. Neither of us believes in the impossible, so we agree that Mrs Spain and her daughter could not have been destroyed by spirits. But how did the murderer escape? There is only one way to find out, and that way must lead us to a definite decision. Let us examine, one by one, all the possible ways of escape. It is clear that the murderer was in the room where Miss Spain was found, or at least in the room joining it, when the people came up the stairs. It is, then, only from these two rooms that we have to find the answer. The police have searched the floors, the ceilings, and the walls, in every direction. So I think we can be sure that nothing could have escaped their attention. But, not trusting their eyes, I examined the place with my own. There were no secret exits. Both doors leading from the rooms into the hall were securely locked, with the keys on the inside. Let us turn to the chimneys. These, in their upper parts, were too narrow even to allow an animal the size of a cat to go through them. It was impossible to escape by any of these means, so we must examine the windows. Through those in the front room, no one could have escaped without attracting the notice of the crowd in the street. The murderers must have gone, then, through the windows in the back room. Now, since we must accept this, we cannot refuse to believe it just because it seems impossible.

'There are two windows in the back room. One of them is clearly visible and has nothing in front of it. The lower part of the other one is hidden from view by the head of a bed which is pushed up against it. The former was found securely fastened from the inside. None of the people who tried could raise it. A large nail had been banged right through both frames, making it impossible to raise the window. The other window was examined, a similar nail was seen fitted in it, and an attempt to raise this window also failed. The police now believed that escape had not been through the window. And, therefore, it was not thought necessary to remove the nails and open the windows.

'My own examination was more careful, because I knew that I must prove that it was possible to escape through the windows.'

A hidden spring

'I therefore began to think that the murderer did escape from one of these windows. This being so, he could not have re-fastened the windows from the inside, as they were found fastened. The windows, therefore, must fasten themselves. I stepped to the window, took out the nail with some difficulty, and tried to raise the window. As I thought, I could not. A hidden spring, I now knew, must exist — a spring, which would allow the window to close by itself. If I could find it, then I was sure my reasoning about the windows would be correct. A careful search soon led to the discovery of the hidden spring. I pressed it, and, satisfied with the discovery, did not bother to raise the window.

'I now replaced the nail and looked at it carefully. A person escaping through this window might have re-closed it, and the spring would have caught. But the nail could not have been replaced. It was obvious that the murderer must have escaped through the other window.

If the springs upon each window were the same, then there had to be a difference between the nails, or at least between the way they went into the frames. Climbing onto the bed, I looked closely at the other window. I easily discovered the spring, which was, as I had thought, exactly the same as that on the first window. I now looked at the nail. It was as strong as the other, and seemed to be fitted in the same manner, driven in deeply, nearly up to the head.

' "There must be something wrong," I thought to myself, "about that nail." I touched it, and the head moved slightly. I pulled at it, and it came off in my fingers with about a quarter of an inch of the length of the nail. The rest of the nail was still in the frame of the window, where it had been broken off. The break was an old one, for around the nail's edges was a reddish powder — rust. I now carefully replaced the head of the nail from where I had taken it, and it looked as if a perfect nail was in place. One could not see that the nail was in fact broken, and of no use at all. Pressing the spring, I gently raised the window for a few inches. The head of the nail went up with it, remaining firm in its place. I closed the window, and the nail appeared whole again.

'The problem was solved. The murderer had escaped through the window which was behind the bed. The window had dropped down by itself after the murderer had escaped, and been fastened by the spring. The police had not known about the spring. They had seen the nail, and thought that that was keeping the window in place.'

How did the murderer climb down?

'The next question is "How did the murderer climb down?" On this point, I had been satisfied in my walk with you around the building. About five and a half feet from the window there is a drain-pipe. From this drain-pipe it would have been impossible for anyone to reach the

window itself, and
to enter through it. I noticed,
however, that the shutters of the
fourth floor were in the form of an ordinary
door (a single, not a folding door), and that the horizontal   5
boards of wood which made the shutter were wide
enough apart to allow an excellent hold for the hands.
When we saw the shutters of the two windows at the back
of the house, they were both about half open. It was clear
to me, that the shutter belonging to the window behind   10
the bed, would, if swung back fully to the wall, reach to
within two feet of the drain-pipe. It was also clear that a
person who was brave enough and agile enough could
have got into the house by reaching from the drain-pipe
to the shutter, then holding onto the shutter and swinging   15
round to the window. And, if we imagine that the window
was open at the time, he might even have swung himself
directly into the room.

'I want you to remember that I have spoken of a very
unusual amount of agility necessary to succeed in doing   20
all this. An ordinary person could not have done it. Added
to this, there is that very peculiar high (or harsh) and
unequal voice. No two persons could be found to agree
about the language that the voice was speaking, and it
could not be understood by anyone at all.'   25

My friend went on.

'You will see,' he said, 'that I have moved from the question of how this person escaped, to how he entered. I intended to show that both were achieved in the same manner, from the same point.

'Let us now turn our attention to the inside of the room. Everything was in a mess, but nothing of real value appeared to have been stolen. The gold francs were still in the bags, which were found on the floor. So the gold could not have been the reason for the murder.

'Remembering the points to which I have drawn your attention — that peculiar voice, the unusual amount of agility needed to get into the house, and the strange absence of a reason for a murder so horrible as this, let us turn to the murder itself. Here is a woman strangled to death by unusual physical strength, and pushed up a chimney, head downward. Ordinary murderers do not do that. You have to admit that there is something here that does not seem to fit in with our normal idea of human behaviour, even when we think about the most terrible of men. Think, too, how strong the murderer must have been to push the body up the chimney so hard that it took several people to drag it down again!

'Turn now to other examples of enormous strength. In front of the fireplace were thick bunches of grey human hair. These had been torn out by the roots. You know how great is the force necessary to tear out even twenty or thirty hairs together. The throat of the old lady had not just been cut, but the head very nearly cut from the body. The instrument was a mere razor. I shall not pay any attention to the bruises upon Mrs Spain's body, though. They must have been caused when the body dropped from the window on to the stone pavement below.

'If now, in addition to all these things, you have thought about the odd disorder of the room, we have the ideas of amazing ability in climbing and jumping, superhuman

strength, a wild murder without any reason, a strange and
horrible scene, and a voice foreign in tone to men of many
nations. What, then, is the result? What effect has my
reasoning had upon you?'

I felt frightened as Dupin asked me this question. 'A
madman,' I said, 'has done this. Someone who escaped
from a neighbouring mad-house.'

The murderer was not human

'In some ways,' he replied, 'your idea is quite close. But
the voices of madmen, even when they are most wild,
never sound like that peculiar voice heard upon the stairs.
Madmen are of some nation, and their language, however
impossible it is to understand the words, always has a
definite pattern. Besides, the hair of a madman is not like
that which I now hold in my hand. I took this little piece
from the fingers of Mrs Spain. Tell me what you can make
of it.'

'Dupin,' I said, horrified, 'this hair is most unusual. This
is not human hair.'

'I have not said that it is,' he said, 'but, before we decide
this point, I want you to look at this little drawing I have
done on this piece of paper. It is a copy of the drawing
made by the police doctor of the dark bruises, and deep
finger marks that were found on Miss Spain's throat. You
will notice,' said my friend, spreading out the paper on
the table in front of us, 'that this drawing gives the idea
of a firm and fixed hold. The hand did not slip. Each finger
was kept, possibly until the death of the victim, in exactly
the same place where it first held Miss Spain's throat. Try
now to place all your fingers, at the same time, in the
same positions as you see them.'

I tried without success.

'We are possibly not giving this matter a fair trial,' he
said. 'The paper is spread out upon a flat surface, but the

human throat is round. Here is a piece of wood, which is about the same thickness as a throat. Wrap the drawing around it, and try the experiment again.'

5   I did so, but the difficulty was even more obvious than before. 'This,' I said, 'is not the mark of a human hand.'

'Now read from this book,' replied Dupin.

Was the murderer an ape?

The book gave a detailed description of the orang-utan from Indonesia. The huge size, strength, and agility of
10   these animals, and their ability to imitate people, is well-known to all. Suddenly I understood the full horrors of the murders.

'The description of the fingers,' I said, as I finished reading, 'agrees exactly with this drawing. I see that no
15   animal but an orang-utan could have made these marks as you have copied them. This piece of hair, too, is exactly as it is described in the book. But I still cannot understand the details of this frightful mystery. Besides, there were two voices heard arguing, and one of them was without
20   doubt the voice of a Frenchman.'

'True, and you will remember that all the witnesses heard the words "My God!" coming from this Frenchman. I am sure these two words will lead us to a full understanding of what happened. A Frenchman knew
25   about the murder. I believe that he was innocent of the terrible events which took place. The orang-utan may have escaped from him. He may have followed it to that room, but, because of what happened, he was probably unable to capture it again. It is still free. I will not continue
30   these guesses, for I have no right to call them more than that. If the Frenchman is indeed innocent of the murder, this advertisement which I left last night at the newspaper office, will bring him to our house. The paper deals with shipping news, and is much read by sailors.'

Dupin's advertisement

He handed me a piece of paper, and I read the following:

> *Caught in nearby woods, early in the morning of*
> *the —* [the morning of the murder], *a very large,*
> *reddish-brown orang-utan from Indonesia. The*   5
> *owner, who is believed to be a sailor working on a*
> *ship from Malta, may have the animal again after*
> *he has proved that it is his, and has paid for the*
> *cost of capturing and keeping it. Call at No. _____ ,*
> *Street _____* [our own address].   10

'How was it possible,' I asked, 'that you could know
that the man is a sailor, and that he works on a ship from
Malta?'

'I do not know it,' said Dupin. 'I am not sure of it. Here,
however, is a small piece of ribbon, which has, I think,   15
been used to tie back hair, in the style which sailors
usually wear. Besides, this knot in the ribbon is a difficult
one which normally only sailors can tie, and only the
Maltese use. I picked up the ribbon in the yard at the back
of the house, at the foot of the drain-pipe. It could not   20
have belonged to either of the two dead women. Now, if
I am wrong in my reasoning about this ribbon, that the
Frenchman was a sailor from a Maltese ship, I can still
have done no harm in saying what I did in the
advertisement. If I am wrong, he will only think that I   25
have misunderstood something, and he will not take the
trouble to ask why. But if I am right, a great point is
gained. Knowing about the murder, though innocent of it,
the Frenchman will naturally hesitate in replying to the
advertisement and demanding the orang-utan. He will   30
think like this: "I am innocent. I am poor. My orang-utan
is of great value, almost worth a fortune to me, so why
should I not take this last chance to get it back? The animal
was found in an area a long way from the scene of the

crime. And anyway, how could it ever be thought that an
animal was the murderer? Above all, someone knows me.
The advertiser describes me as the owner of the animal.
I am not sure how much he knows. If I don't say the
5   animal belongs to me, it will look suspicious because he
knows it is mine. I do not want to attract attention either
to myself or to the orang-utan. I will answer the
advertisement, get the orang-utan, and keep it hidden until
this matter has been forgotten." '

10   At that moment we heard footsteps on the stairs.

'Be ready,' said Dupin, 'with your gun, but don't use it
until I give the signal.'

The sailor arrives

The front door of the house had been left open, and the
15   visitor had entered without ringing the door bell. Now,
however, he seemed to hesitate. But soon we heard him
moving up the stairs in the hall. Dupin moved quickly to
the door and opened it.

'Come in,' said Dupin, in a cheerful tone.

20   A man entered. He was obviously a sailor: a tall, well-
built, strong-looking person. His face, very sunburnt, was
half hidden by a large beard. He bowed awkwardly, and
said good evening. The way he spoke showed that he
was from Paris.

25   'Sit down, my friend,' said Dupin. 'I think you have
come about the orang-utan. He is a very fine animal. How
old do you think he is?'

The sailor took a long breath, as though to calm himself,
and replied, 'I have no way of telling — he can't be more
30   than four or five years old. Have you got him here?'

'Oh no, we couldn't keep him here. He is at a farm
nearby. You can get him in the morning. I shall be sorry
to part with him.'

'I don't want you to go to all this trouble for nothing,
35   sir,' said the man. 'I couldn't expect it. I'm very willing to

pay a reward for the finding of the animal. That is to say, anything within reason.'

'Well,' replied my friend, 'that is all very fair, I'm sure. Let me think, what should I have? Oh! I will tell you. My reward shall be this. You shall give me all the information you can about the murders in the Street of Death.'

Dupin said the last words in a very low tone, and very quietly. Just as quietly, too, he walked toward the door, locked it, and put the key in his pocket. He then drew out his gun, and placed it, quite calmly, on the table.

The sailor looked both angry and frightened. He jumped to his feet and held up the thick stick which he had been carrying when he walked in. But then the next moment he fell back into his chair, shaking badly. He did not speak a word. I pitied him from the bottom of my heart.

'My friend,' said Dupin, in a kind voice, 'you are worrying yourself unnecessarily. We mean you no harm at all. I know perfectly well that you are innocent of the murder that happened there. You cannot, however, deny that you are in some ways involved. From what I have already said, you must know that I have information about this matter. Now, the situation stands like this. You have done nothing which could have been avoided. You were not even guilty of robbery. You have nothing to hide. On the other hand, you should tell us all that you know. An innocent man is now being held by the police. They think he is the murderer, and you know he is not.'

The sailor confesses

The sailor recovered, while Dupin spoke. After a brief pause he said, 'I will tell you all I know. But I do not expect you to believe half of what I say, I would be a
5   fool if I did. Still, I am innocent, and I will tell the truth about it, even if I die for it.'

What he said was, briefly, this. He had recently been to Indonesia. He and several others visited one of the islands, and went into the forest on a pleasure trip. He
10   and one other companion had captured the orang-utan. The companion died soon afterwards, leaving him the owner of the animal. After great trouble during the journey back to France, for the animal was very wild and fierce, the sailor at last took it to his home in Paris. He kept it
15   there, carefully hidden from his neighbours so as to avoid their unpleasant curiosity. He intended to keep it with him until it had recovered from a wound in its foot, then he planned to sell it.

Returning home very late one night from a party with
20   his sailor friends, he found the animal in his bedroom. It had broken out of its cage. Razor in hand, with soap on its face, it was sitting before a mirror, trying to shave. It was obviously trying to copy its master, whom it had watched from its cage many times.

25   Terrified at seeing such a dangerous weapon in a wild animal's hand, the man did not know what to do for some moments. He had always managed to quieten the creature before, by using a whip, so he went and got it. At the sight of the whip, the orang-utan ran through the door of
30   the room, down the stairs, and from there through an open window into the street.

The sailor followed in despair. The ape, razor still in hand, occasionally stopped to look back at his master, following behind. In this manner, the sailor chased the
35   animal for a long time. The streets were very quiet, as it was nearly three o'clock in the morning. They were

passing down a back street, near the street now called the 'Street of Death', when the ape's attention was caught by a light coming from the open window of Mrs Spain's room on the fourth floor of her house. Rushing to the building, it saw the drain-pipe, and climbed up it quickly and easily. It grabbed on to the shutter, which was right back against the wall, and swung itself through the window, directly onto the bed.

The whole thing did not even take a minute. The shutter was kicked open again by the orang-utan as it entered the room. The sailor was now certain he would recapture the animal, as it could only escape one way — by climbing back down the drain-pipe. However, he was rather worried about what it might do in the house. The sailor decided he ought to follow the animal and find out. He climbed up the drain-pipe with no difficulty, being a sailor, but he could not get through the window, which was too far to his left. He could only look inside the room. As he did this, he nearly lost his hold through horror. Then those terrible screams arose into the night, and woke the neighbors from their sleep. Mrs Spain and her daughter, dressed in their nightclothes, had been sitting with their backs to the window, and probably had not seen the orang-utan when it first entered.

The ape murders the two women

As the sailor looked in, the huge animal seized Mrs Spain by the hair, and was waving the sharp razor about her throat. The daughter had fainted on the floor. The screams and struggles of the old lady (during which the hair was torn from her head) made the playful orang-utan angry. With one sweep of its arm, it nearly cut her head from her body. The sight of blood made the angry ape even more wild. It rushed to the body of the girl, and picked her up by the throat, squeezing the life out of her. Then it looked wildly about the room, and saw, through the

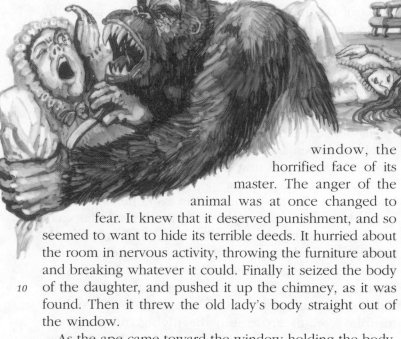

window, the
horrified face of its
master. The anger of the
animal was at once changed to
fear. It knew that it deserved punishment, and so
seemed to want to hide its terrible deeds. It hurried about
the room in nervous activity, throwing the furniture about
and breaking whatever it could. Finally it seized the body
10 of the daughter, and pushed it up the chimney, as it was
found. Then it threw the old lady's body straight out of
the window.

As the ape came toward the window holding the body,
the sailor pressed himself against the drain-pipe, slid down
15 it to the bottom and hurried away home. He was terrified
at what had happened, wanting only to get away as fast
as possible. He completely forgot about trying to capture
the orang-utan. The words heard by the people coming
up the stairs were the Frenchman's exclamations of horror
20 and fear, mixed with the fearful noises of the orang-utan.

I have hardly any more to add. The orang-utan must
have escaped from the room, by the drain-pipe, just before
the police forced open the door. The ape must have
knocked against the window as it passed through it,
25 causing it to drop down and lock itself. The creature was
later caught by its owner, who obtained a large sum of
money for it at a Parisian zoo. The bank clerk was
immediately released after the police had been told the
story of what had really happened.

4

THE LONG BOX

The passenger with three cabins

Some years ago I decided to go by boat to New York. The ship was called the *Independence*, and her Captain was a man named Hardy. I was told that the ship would sail on the fifteenth of the month, if the weather was suitable. On the fourteenth I went on board.

I found that there would be a large number of passengers. I saw several of my friends' names on the passenger list. I was very pleased to see the name Mr C. Wyatt there. We had been close friends when we were students together at university, and he was now a very famous young artist. Wyatt was very clever, but he had the uncertain kind of temper that goes with such cleverness. You could never be sure if he would be in a good mood or a bad mood.

I saw from the list that he had reserved three cabins and that he was travelling with his wife and his two sisters. 'Why,' I wondered to myself, 'does he need three cabins? Surely two would have been enough?' The cabins were big and had two beds in each of them. I knew it was no business of mine and that I should forget the matter, but I could not. I thought of a few reasons why my friend would have reserved three rooms, but they were not good reasons. At last I reached an answer that I should have thought of in the first place. 'It is the servant, of course,' I said to myself. 'What a fool I have been not to have thought of that before!'

Then I looked at the list again, but I could find no servant listed. In fact, I could see quite clearly that he had obviously meant to bring one, but had then changed his

mind, for the words 'and servant' had been written down
and then crossed out. 'Perhaps he has a lot of extra
baggage,' I said to myself, 'something he doesn't want to
put in the baggage room. Perhaps it is a special painting,
5   or something like that.' This idea satisfied my curiosity for
the moment.

A strange delay

I knew Wyatt's two sisters very well, and thought that they
were both clever and attractive. Wyatt had recently
10   married, and I had not yet met his new wife. He had often
talked about her to me though, and from the way he
spoke of her I could see he was deeply in love. He
described her as very beautiful and clever. I was,
therefore, looking forward to meeting her.
15   The day I went to visit the ship, I learned that Wyatt
and his party were also coming on board. I stayed on the
ship for an hour longer than I had meant to, in the hope
of meeting the bride. But then the Captain told me that
he had received a message saying that they would not
20   be coming because Mrs Wyatt was ill. They would not
come on board until the next day, when the ship would
sail.
     The next day, I learned that the Independence would
be a few days late in leaving for New York. Captain Hardy
25   very kindly said he would let me know when everything
was ready. I thought this was rather strange, for the
weather was good. However, the Captain would not say
exactly why the ship was delayed. There was nothing I
could do but go home and wait for the message that
would tell me exactly when we were to leave.

30

I meet Mrs Wyatt

I did not receive the expected message from the Captain
for nearly a week. When I got on board, the ship was

crowded with passengers, and everyone was very busy settling down, getting ready to sail. Wyatt and his group arrived about ten minutes after I did. There were the two sisters, the bride, and the artist. My friend did not seem to be in a good mood. I was so used to his behaviour, though, that I took no notice of this. He did not even introduce me to his wife. His younger sister, Marion, did that. She was a very sweet girl. She quickly saw that her brother did not want to speak to anyone, and so she introduced me to her sister-in-law.

I was amazed when I met Mrs Wyatt. To me, she appeared to be quite a plain woman. She was, however, very well dressed. She said a few polite words to me, and then went into her cabin with her husband.

I was surprised, but I should have remembered how, in the past, my friend's descriptions of beauty had often differed from my own ideas. 'No doubt,' I thought to myself, 'she is so interesting and intelligent that her looks are unimportant.'

The mysterious box

My old curiosity now returned. There was no servant, I could see that. I looked, therefore, for extra baggage. After some time, a cart came to the ship with a long wooden box. This was the only thing that seemed to be expected. Once this box was on board, we started our journey. We had obviously been waiting for it to arrive.

The box was about six feet in length and about two and a half feet wide. I looked at it carefully and decided it was rather a strange shape, but it could, I thought, be suitable for packing pictures in. In fact, I thought I had guessed the contents of that long box correctly, and I was very pleased with myself. Wyatt must have painted a very fine picture and was hoping to get it to New York without telling anyone. I decided that I would ask him about it before the journey was over.

One thing rather annoyed me, though. The box did not
go into the extra cabin. It went into Wyatt's. It must have
taken up a great deal of space and have got in the way
of the artist and his wife.

5   I also noticed that the box was addressed to the artist's
mother-in-law. Although this seemed rather odd, I decided
Wyatt had addressed the box in that way so as to confuse
people like myself. But what I thought really strange was
that the paint used to write the address had a very strong,
10   unpleasant smell. I did not understand how Wyatt or his
wife could bear to have that awful box in their cabin with
them.

An unhappy marriage

For the first three days, we had fine weather. The
15   passengers were well and gay. Only Wyatt and his sisters
were stiff and unfriendly. I thought they were rather bad-
mannered. I tried to get them to talk to some of my other
friends, but nothing I could do had any effect.

Mrs Wyatt herself was much more friendly. She talked
20   quite happily with all the other ladies about this and that.
She amused us all very much. I was also rather astonished
by her, for I had been led to believe that she was very
clever. The truth was, I soon found out, that people often
laughed at Mrs Wyatt. The gentlemen did not talk much
25   about her, but the ladies, after a while, began to say that
she was, 'A good little thing, not very pretty, totally
uneducated, and rather stupid.' I wondered how Wyatt
had been trapped into marrying such a person. I thought
that perhaps she was very rich, but then I remembered
30   that Wyatt had told me that she had no money of her own
and she never expected to have any. 'I married for love,'
he had told me, 'and for love only.'

When I thought about this, I was very puzzled. Could
it be possible that he was going mad? What else could I
35   think? Certainly the lady seemed very fond of him. She

was always talking about him when he was not with her. In fact she often made herself look quite stupid by so often repeating what her 'dear husband' had said. She was always using the word 'husband'. In the meantime, everyone on board noticed that Wyatt avoided his wife whenever he could, and, whenever possible, he shut himself up in his cabin alone. The other passengers could see that the marriage was not a success.

I pitied Wyatt from the bottom of my heart, because he was an old friend. I could not understand why he had married this young woman. But even though I was sorry for him, I could still not forgive him for refusing to tell me about the painting that I thought he had in that long box. I was determined to question him about it.

Wyatt seems to be going mad

One day he came up on deck. I took his arm and began walking with him around the boat. He seemed to be rather unhappy, which didn't surprise me. He didn't say much. I tried to make a joke, and he made a weak effort to smile. Poor man! I thought of his wife and realized that he did not have much to smile about. At last I decided to mention the box. I said something about the strange shape of the box, and as I did so, I gave him a knowing smile and touched his arm gently.

The way Wyatt behaved towards what I thought was a harmless joke made me think that he was definitely going mad. At first he stared at me as if he found it impossible to understand. Then, as the point seemed to slowly make its way to his brain, his eyes looked as though they would come right out of his head. His face grew very red, then, suddenly, quite pale. Then he began to laugh loudly, and he continued to laugh for about ten minutes. At the end of all this, he fell flat and heavily onto the deck. When I tried to lift him up, he was so lifeless that I thought he was dead.

I called for help, and after we had got him to a chair, he began to recover. At first he spoke to himself for some
5   time and no one could understand what he was saying. But we managed to quieten him, take him to his cabin, and put him to bed. The next morning he was quite well again, at least in
10   body. About his mind, I was not so sure.

I avoided him during the rest of the journey. The Captain had advised me to do so. I think he believed that I was in some way responsible for Wyatt's near madness. He also warned me to say nothing about Wyatt's
15   behaviour to any of the other passengers.

Not long after this event, something else happened which made me even more curious about Wyatt's family life and that strange-shaped box.

I had been sleeping badly for two or three nights, and
20   I usually left my cabin door open because the cabin became very hot. When the door was open, I could see quite clearly the doors of the cabins where Wyatt and his wife and sisters were. During the nights that I didn't sleep, I clearly saw Mrs Wyatt come quietly out of her husband's
25   cabin at about eleven o'clock each time, and enter the extra room. She stayed in that extra cabin until morning, when she was called by her husband and went back.

It was clear to me that the marriage was a very unhappy one. It seemed that they were almost separated. And so I learnt about the mystery of the extra cabin.

The sound of quiet crying

There was one other thing which interested me very much. On those same nights that I saw Mrs Wyatt going to the extra cabin, I also heard some strange sounds coming from Wyatt's cabin.

After listening carefully to these sounds for some time, I decided that I knew what they were. They were the sounds made by the artist opening the box. I could hear him taking off the top and carefully laying it down. After that there was a dead stillness, and I could hear nothing more until nearly morning.

There was one other sound I heard, although it was so soft I might have imagined it. It seemed to be the sound of quiet crying, almost like sighing, but of course it could not have been either. I could see no reason for my friend Wyatt to be crying over some beautiful painting.

Just before dawn, on each of the two nights of which I speak, I clearly heard Wyatt replace the lid on the box, and force the nails into their old places with a hammer. He softened the noise by covering the hammer with some kind of cloth. Having done this, he came out of his cabin, fully dressed, and brought Mrs Wyatt from her cabin back to his.

A terrible storm

We had been at sea seven days when a terrible storm suddenly blew up. We managed to sail through it quite well for about forty-eight hours. At the end of that, though, the storm was too strong for our poor ship. Water raced over the sides, and three men were lost. We lost our sails and everything was looking very bad. The ship was taking in a lot of water. One of the sailors told the Captain that there was four feet of water in the bottom of the boat. 'The pumps won't work, either,' he said.

5 There was confusion everywhere. Only the Captain remained calm. He soon got a team of men together and ordered them to throw out as much heavy baggage as they could find, in order to make the ship as light as possible. We did what we could, but the pumps still wouldn't work and the water in the ship was rising fast.

10 At the end of the day, as the sun was setting, the weather grew calmer. The sea grew quieter. We knew that the *Independence* could not be saved, but we thought that we might now be able to lower the small boats. At eight o'clock that evening, the full moon came out and gave us 15 a good light to see by. It cheered our low spirits a lot, seeing that bright, clear moon.

After much hard work, we managed to get one of the boats over the side. Into this we put all of the crew and most of the passengers. The boat was set free from the 20 *Independence* as quickly as possible, and finally landed safely on the mainland about three days later.

Fourteen passengers and the Captain remained on board. We let down another boat without difficulty. Into it, we put the Captain and his wife, Wyatt and his party, 25 a Mexican officer with his wife and four children, and myself.

'Let me have my box'

We had no room, of course, for anything except the most necessary things. There was enough food for a few days, 30 water, and the clothes we were wearing, and that was all. No one had even thought of trying to take more. Imagine our astonishment, then, when, after we had gone a few feet from the *Independence*, Mr Wyatt stood up in that little boat and demanded that Captain Hardy should return 35 to the ship and get his long box, which he had left behind!

'Sit down, Mr Wyatt,' replied the Captain sternly, 'or you will turn the boat over and we will all drown.'

'The box!' said Mr Wyatt, still standing. 'The box! You must do as I ask! It does not weigh very much; nothing at all, really. Please, please, let me have my box!'   5

The artist looked so upset that, for a moment, the Captain seemed to weaken, but then he recovered his stern manner, and said, 'Mr Wyatt, you are mad. I cannot listen to you. Sit down, I say, or you will cause us all to die.'   10

Wyatt did not seem to hear, and, as the Captain shouted to the rest of us to try to stop him, the young artist jumped from the boat.

He swam, with almost superhuman strength, back to the *Independence*, and we saw him climb back on board   15 with the help of a rope that was hanging over the side. In the meantime, we had been swept further away from the *Independence*.

Wyatt throws himself into the sea

As our distance from the sinking ship increased, the   20 madman (for we could only think of him as mad) reappeared at the top of the steps leading down to the cabins. He was dragging that long box with him. While we watched him with astonishment, he tied a thick rope first round the box and then around his own body. In another moment, both the box and Wyatt were in the sea, and then they disappeared, suddenly, at once and forever.

5   We waited there silently for a few moments, staring at the spot where the artist had disappeared. At last we moved away. No one spoke for an hour or more. Finally I decided to say something.

'Did you notice, Captain, how suddenly they sank?
10   Don't you think that was rather odd? I must say, that when I saw him tie himself to that box, I thought he might be saved. I thought he might be able to float on the box to safety.'

'It was quite natural that that box should sink so fast'
15   replied the Captain. 'They will soon rise again, however, but not until the salt melts.'

'The salt!' I exclaimed.

'Hush!' said the Captain, pointing to the wife and the sisters of the drowned man. 'We must talk of these things
20   at some other time.'

We suffered a lot, and had a narrow escape from death, but fortune smiled on us in that small boat. We landed, in the end, more dead than alive, after four days of terror, never knowing if we were going to live or die. We landed
25   at a village on the mainland and stayed there, with the villagers, for about a week. Then we caught another boat that was going to New York.

The truth of the matter

About a month after the loss of the *Independence*, I
30   happened to meet Captain Hardy in New York. Our conversation turned, naturally, to what had happened to the *Independence*, and, to what had happened to poor Wyatt. I learned the following things:

The artist had reserved cabins for himself, his wife, his
35   two sisters and a servant. His wife was, indeed, as he had

described her, a most lovely and intelligent woman. On the morning of 14th June, the day I had first visited the ship, the lady suddenly became ill and died. The young husband was so sad that at first he did not know what to do. But he had to go to New York. He then decided to take the body of his dear wife with him, back to her mother in New York, but he knew that it would be impossible to do this if he told anyone about it. Almost all the passengers and probably most of the crew would have refused to go on a ship that was carrying a dead body.

Wyatt told Captain Hardy of his problem. The Captain, being a good friend of Wyatt's, decided what to do. He arranged for the body to be packed, with a large quantity of salt, in a long box. It was then taken on board as ordinary cargo.

Nothing was to be said about the lady dying, and, since it was well-known that Mr Wyatt was to be travelling with his wife, it was necessary to find someone who could pretend to be her during the sea journey. The maid was persuaded to do this. The extra cabin, meant for this girl in the first place, was kept so as not to cause suspicion. The maid-wife slept in there every night. In the daytime she tried, as well as she could, to play the part of Mrs Wyatt. It was a lucky thing that none of the passengers had ever met Mr Wyatt's new wife.

My own mistakes arose, naturally enough, through being too careless, too curious, and too ready to think I had found the right answer.

Knowing the truth of the matter, I rarely sleep well now. I often see the face of my poor dead friend and hear his terrible laugh.

5

SOME WORDS WITH A MUMMY

An invitation

I had a bad headache and felt very sleepy. I had intended to go out that evening, but I decided against it. Instead, I thought I would have a light supper and go to bed.

5 My wife will perhaps tell you that my idea of a light supper is not the same as hers. But all I had were three pieces of cheese pie, washed down with rather a lot of beer. Five bottles, I have to admit, is not a small quantity.

Having finished my 'light' meal, I went up to bed in the
10 hope that I would sleep until late into the next day. I fell asleep almost immediately.

However, I did not get as good a night's sleep as I had hoped. I could hardly have slept for more than half an hour, when the front door bell began to ring very loudly
15 and someone began to knock on the door impatiently. About a minute later, while I was still rubbing my eyes, my wife pushed a note under my nose. It was from my close friend Doctor Ponnonner, and this is what it said:

Come and see me at once, my good friend. Come
20 *and help us all with our good fortune. At last, the managers of the City Museum have agreed to allow me to examine that Egyptian mummy — you know the one I mean. I have permission to cut it open if necessary. Only a few friends will be present. You,*
25 *of course, are included. The mummy is now at my house, and we shall begin examining it at eleven tonight.*

Yours ever,
Ponnonner

By the time I had reached the word 'Ponnonner' I was wide awake. I leaped out of bed in great excitement. I dressed myself as quickly as I could, and rushed off, as fast as possible, to the doctor's home.

When I reached it, I found a number of eager men there. They had been waiting for me with some impatience. The mummy was laid out in its box on the dining-room table. The moment I entered the room, the examination began.

They begin to examine the mummy

The mummy was one of a pair, brought from Egypt several years before. It had been found near the Nile, deep underground, in some richly decorated caves, and had been surrounded by treasure.

The treasure had been given to the City Museum by the man who discovered it, and the mummy had been there too, in its former condition, for eight years. No one had been allowed to touch it or open the box it was in. You can imagine our excitement and pleasure at now being allowed to do this.

Approaching the table, I saw that the mummy was in a large box, nearly seven feet in length, and perhaps three feet wide, and two and a half feet deep. At first we thought the box was made of wood. When we cut it, however, we realized that the material was not wood but a paste-like mixture made from papyrus reeds that grow along the banks of the river Nile. It was decorated with scenes connected with death. There were also some words written in a strange alphabet. Luckily, there was a man called Mr Gliddon among our group. He could understand the ancient Egyptian writing, and was able to tell us what it meant.

We had some difficulty in opening the outer case without causing any damage to what lay inside. At last we did so, and found another, smaller case, almost exactly the same as the first one.

When we had opened this one, which we did quite easily, we saw a third case. This one was made of a sweet-smelling wood.

We removed the third case and found the body inside it. We had expected to find the body wrapped in the normal way, that is, wrapped in long thin pieces of cloth-like bandages. This body, however, was covered in a kind of blanket made of papyrus reeds. The blanket was painted with scenes about the duties of the soul of the dead person. There also appeared to be paintings of different gods, and a number of paintings of the same human figure. We thought these were probably pictures of the dead person, showing what he looked like. There was also some writing which Mr Gliddon told us was a list, giving the mummy's name and titles, and the names of his relatives and their titles.

Around the top of the blanket was a kind of collar of different coloured glass beads, which formed pictures of different gods. Around the middle part of the blanket was a sort of belt, also with pictures on it.

The body

When we removed the blanket, we found the body. It was in excellent condition. It did not smell. The skin was reddish, hard and smooth. The teeth and hair were in good condition. The eyes, it seemed, had been removed, 5 and replaced with what we thought must have been glass ones. They were very beautiful and very life-like, except that they had a fixed stare. The fingers and the nails had been very cleverly painted with some strange Egyptan symbols. 10

We searched the body very carefully for the usual openings through which the parts inside are removed, but we couldn't find any. None of us realized then that a large number of Egyptian mummies are found completely whole. From what we knew at that time, the 15 brain was normally drawn out through the nose. The stomach was drawn out through a cut made in the side of the body. The body was then shaved, washed and completely covered with salt. It was left like that for several weeks, and then it was ready to be preserved for 20 ever.

As we could find none of the openings we expected, Doctor Ponnonner began preparing his instruments in order to cut the body open. I knew this would be a long job, so I pointed out to everyone that it was then past two 25 o'clock in the morning. We decided to continue with our examination the following evening. We were all about to go home, when someone suggested doing an electrical experiment.

We all agreed that this was a wonderful idea, and the 30 thought of sleep went from our minds completely. What we intended to do was to pass an electric current through the mummy and see what happened. We didn't really expect very much, for the mummy was at least three or four thousand years old. I don't know why we were all 35 so excited by the idea.

The eyes change

After a lot of trouble, we succeeded in attaching an electrical wire to one of the muscles in the mummy's head. We had to make a small cut in the forehead to make this
5   possible. When the electricity was turned on, of course, nothing happened. We all laughed at each other, feeling a little stupid and wondering why we had started this experiment anyway. We said good night, and began to leave. Then I looked at the mummy's eyes, and I stared
10 in amazement at what I saw. The eyes no longer looked like glass, and they were now half shut.

With a shout I called attention to the change, and it was immediately noticed by all the others.

I cannot say if I was alarmed at what had happened,
15 because 'alarmed' was not quite the right word for what I was feeling. It is possible, however, that if I had not drunk so much beer earlier in the evening, that is exactly how I would have felt.

The rest of my friends made no attempt to hide their
20 fright. Doctor Ponnonner was so terrified that he became a man to be pitied. Mr Gliddon seemed, somehow, to make himself almost disappear. Mr Buckingham crawled on his hands and knees under the table.

After the first surprise, however, we decided that the
25 best thing to do was to continue our electrical experiments. We decided to see if we could make the right toe move. We made a small cut, and again attached the electrical wire to a muscle in the leg. We then turned on the electric current. With a very life-like movement, the
30 mummy first drew up its right knee, back to the stomach, and then, straightening its leg, it gave Doctor Ponnonner a very heavy kick. The good doctor flew backwards, right out of the window, into the street below.

We rushed out all together, fearful that we would find
35 our friend's broken body on the street. He had suffered no injury, though, and he came quickly up the stairs again,

even more eager to continue the experiment.

Following his advice, therefore, we made a cut on the nose of the mummy. The doctor then attached the wire.

The mummy speaks!

The effect was electric, in more ways than one. Firstly, the mummy opened its eyes. Secondly, it sneezed, and thirdly, it sat up. It then shook its fist at Doctor Ponnonner. It turned to Mr Gliddon and Mr Buckingham, and spoke to them in beautiful Egyptian.

'I must say gentlemen, that I am surprised and upset by your behaviour. I could not expect Doctor Ponnonner to behave well, I suppose. He is a poor fat fool who doesn't know any better. I pity and forgive him. But you, Mr Gliddon, and you, Mr Buckingham, you have both travelled and lived in Egypt and know the language and the customs perfectly. You both read and write Egyptian as well as you do your own language. I have always believed that you have been good to mummies, treating them correctly and well. I really did think that you would behave better than this. How could you stand there and allow me to be treated in this way? How could you allow these strangers to uncover me like this and examine me, as they have done, in such a cold climate? I mean, you actually helped that silly doctor to pull my nose!'

5   You would imagine, when we heard these words coming from what we thought was a dead body, that we would all either rush to the door, or faint, or stand there terrified, unable to move. Any one of these things was to be expected after what we had seen and heard. I cannot

10   explain why none of them happened. Perhaps we did none of these things because of the very normal, natural way in which the mummy spoke. Anyway, whatever the reason, none of us seemed very frightened by these odd happenings.

15   I was sure everything was all right. I stepped back a little so that the mummy's fist could not reach me if he decided to hit me. Doctor Ponnonner put his hands in his trouser pockets and stared very hard at the mummy, and grew very red in the face. Mr Gliddon stroked his chin

20   and drew up the collar of his shirt. Mr Buckingham stared down at the floor and put his finger in his mouth.

A conversation in Ancient Egyptian

The Egyptian looked at Mr Buckingham for some minutes, and then said, 'Why don't you speak, Mr Buckingham? Did

25   you hear what I asked you? Please take your finger out of your mouth!'

At this, Mr Buckingham jumped slightly, took his finger out of his mouth, and then put another finger in the other side of his mouth!

30   Not being able to get an answer from Mr Buckingham, the mummy turned to Mr Gliddon. He asked him very severely what we were all doing.

Mr Gliddon explained in great detail, speaking in very beautiful and correct Ancient Egyptian.

Naturally, all conversation had to be in this language, and Mr Gliddon spoke it well. Whenever any of the others wanted to talk to the mummy, either Mr Gliddon or Mr Buckingham acted as interpreters.

I could not help noticing that the mummy could not understand certain modern words. At one stage, for example, Mr Gliddon could not make the Egyptian understand the word 'politics', for quite a long time.

Mr Gliddon, naturally, in his conversation with the mummy, was most interested in telling him all about modern science, especially how advanced we were in the examination of mummies. Mr Gliddon also apologized for upsetting him, and hinted that he would like to continue examining him.

The mummy accepted Mr Gliddon's apologies, but did not seem at all eager to continue the experiments on himself. Instead he got down from the table and shook hands with all of us.

When he had done this, we immediately repaired the damage he had received during the electrical experiments. We sewed up the wound on his forehead, wrapped a bandage around his foot, and put a small plaster on the cut on his nose. We then noticed that the Count (this, we were told, was the mummy's title) was shivering, no doubt because of the cold.

The doctor immediately went to his wardrobe, and took out a black evening jacket, a pair of blue trousers, a pink shirt, a white raincoat, a hat, a pair of boots and a tie. Because the doctor and the Count were rather different sizes, the doctor being much larger, these clothes looked rather odd on the Egyptian. Once he was dressed, Mr Gliddon led him to a chair by the fire, and we all sat down.

We were, of course, very curious about how the Count still managed to be alive.

'I should have thought,' said Mr Buckingham, 'that you would be dead by now.'

The mummy is 5,750 years old

'Why,' replied the Count, very much astonished, 'I am only just over 700 years old! My father lived 1,000 years. He did not look at all old when he died.'

5   A number of questions and answers followed, for we believed that it was 5,050 years, and a few months, since the Count had been buried. The Count agreed that this was so, but what he meant was that he had been 700 years old when he was buried.

10   Mr Buckingham quickly agreed that the Count indeed still looked like a young man, but what he wanted to know was, after having been dead and buried for over 5,000 years, how could he be with us today, alive and well?

The Count then explained that the medical men of his
15   day had known how to preserve people. We were all astonished by the medical knowledge of the people who lived at his time. They seemed to know much more than us. He then went on to tell us that he had not been buried dead but had been alive. He had had an illness which
20   made him fall into a deep sleep. The doctors could not cure it, and so they thought it best to preserve him as a mummy and bury him.

After a long silence, Doctor Ponnonner spoke, 'It is possible, then,' he said, 'that there might be other
25   mummies along the Nile that were buried in the same way, and they, too, could come alive again.'

'That is absolutely right,' replied the Count. 'All of us who were preserved while still alive, are still alive.'

'Will you be kind enough to explain,' I said, 'why you
30   were preserved while still alive?'

'With great pleasure,' he said. 'In my time a person used to live about 800 years. Few men died, except by accident, before the age of 600. A few lived longer than 1,000 years, but 800 years was considered normal.

35   'After the discovery of how to preserve people, our scientists decided that the writing of history would be

helped if someone from the past could correct the mistakes of modern historians. For example, a historian who is 500 years old writes a book. He then asks to be preserved, and brought back to life after five or six hundred years. Coming to life again after such a length of time, he would find the people of that time had misunderstood his history book, and therefore they would not know the true history of the time about which he wrote. Because he had come alive again, he could correct all their mistakes and tell them what really happened in the time in which he had lived. This process of rewriting history by such historians, who came back to life in a different time from their own, made sure that our history was always true, and never became false.'

'Well,' said Mr Buckingham. 'That is amazing. But surely, Count, the great age to which people lived in your time, and the ability to live again later, must mean that your people had a huge amount of knowledge. If this is so, then why was Egyptian science so poor? We modern people are, I think, far more developed, don't you agree?'

'I am not sure,' said the Count. 'What kinds of science are you talking about?'

The mummy shows his knowledge of science

Here, all of us took our turn in asking him about different scientific discoveries that we believed had only become known in our time. We were disappointed in his answers. He knew everything we knew. He knew about the making of glass, about how the brain and nervous systems worked. He showed us that the ancient Egyptians knew far more about lifting weights and making large buildings than we do. He listed many things, including using steam for power, that left us all feeling very stupid.

Then Doctor Ponnonner spoke up. He asked the Count how he felt about the advances made since his day in the clothing industry.

The Count looked
at the doctor, and
then looked down at
the clothes he was
5 wearing. He felt the
cloth of his trousers
carefully, rubbing it
between his fingers.
Then he felt the material
10 of the shirt. He did the
same with his tie, then he
dropped it. A smile grew on his
face which went from ear to ear.
He did not seem to think it
15 necessary to make any other reply.

Although the questions had not ended
to our advantage, they had ended amusingly,
and we recovered our good mood. Doctor
Ponnonner, however, was not going to allow the mummy
20 to think he was better than us in everything. He went up
to the Count, and asked him to say honestly, if the
Egyptians in his time had ever heard of the medicine
known as Ponnonner's Pills.

We waited anxiously for an answer. There was nothing.
25 The Egyptian hung his head in shame. Never was a victory
more complete. Never was defeat so clear. Indeed, I could
not bear the sight of the poor defeated mummy. I reached
for my hat, bowed to him, and left.

When I got home, I found it was past four o'clock, and
30 I went straight to bed. It is now ten in the morning. I have
been up since seven, writing this story for the good of my
family and for the good of mankind. I will not see my
wife again, but the truth is, I don't mind. Besides, I am
anxious to know who will be President in 2045. Therefore,
35 as soon as I have finished this cup of coffee, I shall go
over to Doctor Ponnonner's house and get myself
preserved for a couple of hundred years.

THE FALL OF THE HOUSE OF USHER

A visit to a sick friend

It was a dull, dark, autumn day. The clouds were lying low in the sky. I was riding alone, and as evening fell I saw for the first time, in front of me, the House of Usher.

I do not know why, but the sight of that house made me feel very uneasy. My happiness vanished. I could find no pleasure in the sight before me. The walls of the house seemed cold and unfriendly. The windows were like cruel eyes. The plants and trees surrounding the house looked unhealthy and lifeless. My heart turned to ice. But I could not understand exactly what made me feel so uneasy when I looked at the House of Usher. I only knew I felt uncomfortable. I stopped my horse at the edge of the black lake that lay, perfectly calm, next to the house. I looked down into its depths. The lake seemed even more frightening than the house itself.

In spite of my feelings towards the House of Usher, I was going to stay there for some weeks. Its owner, Roderick Usher, had been one of my closest companions when I was a boy, but we had not seen each other for many years. Then I had received a totally unexpected letter from him. He said he was physically very ill and also had a mental disorder. He said he thought that seeing me, his best and only personal friend, would help to make him feel happier.

Although, as boys, we had been close friends, I felt that I really knew very little about Roderick Usher. He had always been very quiet and never had much to say about himself. I knew, however, that his ancient family was well known for its wealth and goodness.

I had also learned that although the Usher family was an old one, there were no living relatives outside the immediate family. The family name and possessions always went directly from father to son. Perhaps because of this, the house became known by the same name as the family — the House of Usher.

Dark rooms and halls

I had been standing at the edge of the lake in a kind of dream. I tried to shake off my uneasy feelings. I looked
15 at the house more carefully. It was very old indeed. Plants climbed over the walls, and the building looked uncared-for. Some of the stones seemed to be loose in their foundations. I wondered if the wood in the building was rotten also. I felt that if I examined the walls I would find
20 a crack going from the high roof all the way down the walls that ended at the edge of the lake. I also wondered how deep the cellars under the house were, and if, in fact, they went right under the lake.

Thinking these dark thoughts, I rode over the bridge
25 and crossed to the other side of the lake. A servant took my horse; another led me to the master of the house. We passed through many dark rooms and halls. On one of the staircases I met the family doctor. I did not like the look of him at all. He introduced himself quickly and then
30 went on his way.

At last we reached my friend's room. It was very large, with a high ceiling. The windows were long, narrow and pointed. They were so narrow that very little light entered the room. The pictures on the wall were dark and uninteresting. There was a lot of furniture in the room, all old, dark and uncomfortable, and in bad repair. There were many books and musical instruments lying around, but they did not give me the feeling that their owner had any real love for them. I felt that I was standing in a room of great sorrow.

Roderick Usher has changed

As I entered, Usher rose from a sofa where he had been lying, and greeted me warmly. Although I felt that his greeting was perhaps too warm, his face convinced me that he meant every word he had said in his letter. We sat down, and for some moments I looked at him with sadness mixed with wonder. He had changed so much. I could hardly recognize my friend Roderick Usher. He was very, very pale. His eyes were unnaturally large and liquid. His lips were beautifully curved, but rather thin. His nose was well formed, as was his chin, although it was a bit too small for a man of character and strength. His forehead was wide, and his hair beautifully soft. It was a face that could not be easily forgotten. But over all this lay so much change that I doubted that the man before me was really my friend at all. Every part of his face told of some terrible worry and fear.

I remembered certain things of my friend, when he was a boy, that I could still recognize in the man in front of me. He was very nervous. He often went from being very happy and excited to being very quiet and dull. His voice changed quickly from being weak and uncertain to being strong and sure. When he became very excited it was difficult to understand him at all. In these ways, Roderick Usher had not changed.

A family evil

He spoke to me excitedly, now, of the purpose of my visit, of his desire to see me, and how happy he thought he would be. He told me, at great length, of what he
5   thought his illness was. It was, he said, a physical illness, but one that had always been a family evil, and one which could not be cured. The illness made him very nervous. He found it difficult to eat anything except very simple food. Rough clothing made his skin itch terribly. His eyes
10 had become weak, and strong light would give him a bad headache. The scent of flowers made him feel sick. The sounds from musical instruments filled him with terror.

So nervous had he become, that he imagined danger round every corner. He seemed to feel that he was fighting
15 against a 'thing' that he could name only as 'fear'.

I also learned of another feeling that gave some hint of his strange mental condition. It was the house itself. He had lived there for many years without ever going outside, and now he felt trapped by its grey walls. The very
20 darkness of the place, the building and the lake had had a terrible effect on my friend's feelings.

The Lady Madeline

He did say, though, that much of his strange behaviour could have been caused by the severe and long illness of
25 his very dear sister. This sister had been his only companion for many years. She was his last living relation.

'When she dies,' he said, with a terrible sadness, 'I will be the only living member of the ancient family of the Ushers.'
30 While he spoke, the Lady Madeline, his sister, passed slowly through the other end of the room. She did not seem to notice me, and disappeared without saying anything. I looked at her with mixed feelings of astonishment and fear. But I could not say why. A terrible

feeling came
over me as I watched
her disappear. As soon as she had gone
I turned to face her brother, but he had buried his face
in his hands. I could see his tears falling through his   5
fingers.

Lady Madeline's illness had puzzled her doctors for a
long time. She had steadily become weaker and weaker.
On the very evening of my arrival at the House of Usher,
she was forced to go to her bed. She was no longer strong   10
enough to walk around. I learned from her brother that
the brief sight I had had of her would be the last time I
would see her. From now on, she would stay in her room
and see no visitors.

For several days after this, neither Usher nor myself   15
mentioned her name. I spent my whole time trying to
cheer up my friend. We painted and read together.
Sometimes I listened to him playing strange music on his
guitar. While I listened, I watched him closely. I could see
that his moments of happiness with me were only   20
moments. His true condition was still one of terrible
despair.

I shall always remember the many long hours I spent alone with the master of the House of Usher. Yet I cannot explain exactly what we did or talked about, or what he showed me. I remember only a few things. His long
5 excited speeches will ring in my ears for ever, and yet I cannot remember what those speeches were about. I remember listening to wild music. I remember that the pictures he painted terrified me, yet what they meant, I do not know.

10 ## Roderick's sister is dead

One evening, Usher told me that his sister had died. He said that he intended to preserve her body for a fortnight in one of the cellars under the house, before she was finally taken to her grave. He said he was going to do this
15 so that some of her doctors, who had been confused by the disease, would have a chance to examine her body again. I felt this was quite sensible. I had not liked the look of the doctor I had seen, and thought that examinations by other doctors might help explain why she
20 had died.

Usher asked me to help him move his sister's body. The cellar where the dead body was placed was small, damp and dark. It had the smell of places that have been closed up for a long time. It had no windows, and the only light
25 came from the two candles we carried. It was directly underneath my own room.

For the first time I saw how much Lady Madeline looked like her brother. Usher, perhaps realizing my thoughts, told me that they were twins, and had always been very
30 close. We did not stay down there long. We closed the heavy door of the cellar and returned upstairs.

Some days later, I noticed that a complete change had come over the face of my friend. His normal manner had disappeared. He hurried from room to room for no reason.

He had become even paler than before. His eyes had lost their unnatural shine and become very dull. His voice grew high when he spoke, as though he was unable to control it. Sometimes I thought he was trying to build up the courage to tell me what was upsetting him. At other times I thought he was going mad. Sometimes I caught him staring into nothing, with his head bent to one side as though he were listening for some kind of sound. It was not surprising that his condition terrified me. The terror grew on me like a disease. The strangeness of Usher's behaviour was having its effect on me.

Usher has seen something

One night, about six or seven nights after we had placed Lady Madeline in the cellar, I felt the full strength of the feelings of terror that had grown in me. I could not sleep. I tried to fight the nervousness that I felt. I tried to make myself believe that it was the dark furniture in the room, the strange paintings on the walls and the torn curtains that had upset me. But it was no good. I was becoming more frightened every minute. Then terrible sounds reached my ears: strange, low, frightening sounds. I could not tell where they came from. I got up quickly and dressed, for I knew I would not be able to sleep. In order to keep warm and to try to quieten my mind, I walked back and forth across my room.

I had been doing this for a few minutes, when I heard light steps on the staircase leading to my room. After a few moments, I recognized the steps as those of Usher. Then, he was at my door, knocking nervously. I called to him to come in.

At the sound of my voice he entered, carrying a lamp. He was, as usual, very pale, but this time there was something different about his eyes. There was the light of madness in them.

He looked terrible, but anything was better than the dreadful loneliness that I had just been through. I even welcomed him with real joy.

'Haven't you seen it?' he said suddenly, after looking
5 about for some moments in silence. 'You haven't seen it, then? But wait, you shall.' Saying these words, he carefully put down the lamp he was carrying and rushed to open one of the windows.

Outside the wind blew strongly, and as the window
10 flew open we were nearly blown off our feet. It was a wild but beautiful night. Clouds flew all over the sky and even seemed to be trying to push against the highest parts of the house.

'You must not excite yourself like this,' I said, shaking.
15 I quickly led Usher away from the window to a chair. 'We must close the window. The cold air will do you serious harm. Look. Here is one of your favourite books. Shall I read it?'

Frightening noises

I sat down and started to read. I hoped that the sound of my steady voice might calm him. Outside the wind grew
20 stronger and we could see flashes of lightning and hear violent thunder. My story had reached the stage where the hero had not been allowed to enter the house of a friend. He was so angry that he beat the door down. As he did this, the most dreadful screaming was heard and the hero
25 had to cover his ears with his hands against the sound, it was so terrible.

As I reached that part of the story, I stopped reading. I looked up from my book with wild amazement, for I could hear the very same sounds that I had been reading
30 about. I could not tell where the sounds came from exactly, but I thought that they came from far away, lower down in the house.

Although I was very frightened by what I had heard, I still had enough sense not to excite my companion by showing him I was upset. I was not even sure if he had heard those strange noises, although I thought his expression had changed.

Usher gradually turned his chair until he was facing the door of the room. I could then only see his face from the side. I saw that his lips were trembling. His head dropped, but I knew he was not asleep. His eyes were open wide and staring. His body rocked from side to side, as though he were in pain. I decided it would be best if I continued to read:

'The hero looked round quickly for some kind of weapon. He saw a huge shining shield on the wall and went to pull it down. In his struggle to get the shield off the wall it came crashing onto the floor, making a great ringing sound.'

No sooner had I read out these words than I heard sounds exactly like those of a shield being dropped heavily on the floor. Terrified, I leapt to my feet. Usher did not stop his rocking. His eyes were staring straight in front of him. I placed my hand on his shoulder, and asked him if he hadn't heard the noise, too. His whole body shook. He started to speak in a low, quick whisper. Bending over him, I at last understood the horrible meaning of his words.

Lady Madeline is at the door

'Not hear it? Yes, I heard it. I have heard noises from down there for many long minutes and many long hours. Yet I dared not, oh pity me, poor fool that I am! I did not dare to speak! She was living when we put her in the cellar! I have heard her weakly moving about down there for many, many days. Yet I did not dare to speak. That story you read. The breaking down of the door. You should say

that it was her
trying to break down the
door of the cellar, and struggling
against the iron locks! Oh where, where
shall I go? Haven't I heard her footsteps on the
stairs? Can't I hear the beating of her heart? Oh, this is
driving me mad. I am a madman!' At this point he jumped
wildly to his feet and screamed out his words, as if in the
effort he were giving up his soul. 'I am a madman! I tell
10 you she is now standing at the door!'

As if his words had been given power, the huge door
drew slowly open. I thought for a moment the wind had
blown it open. But had it? There on the other side of the
door stood the figure of the Lady Madeline of Usher. There
15 was blood on her white robes. There was evidence of
some terrible struggle on every part of her thin body. For
a moment she remained there, trembling. Then, with a
low cry, she fell upon him, and dragged him with her to
the floor. He was dead, dead from terror. My friend died
20 a victim of the terrors of the House of Usher.

The house is destroyed

I ran from that room and away from the house in wild, mad horror. I rushed out across the bridge. The storm was still roaring all around me. Suddenly, a light shone along the path. I turned to see where it could have come from.   5

Behind me stood the huge old house and its dark shadows. There was nothing else. The light came from the full moon, which now shone strongly through the outline of the ancient house. Then, while I looked, I saw the crack. Before, I had only thought of a crack, but now it   10 was there. It stretched through the building, from roof to lake. It rapidly grew wider and wider until the whole house began to break up as I watched.

My brain rocked as I saw the great walls crashing down. There was an unbelievably loud noise, like the sound of a thousand rivers rushing down the side of a mountain. And then, at my feet, the waters of the deep, dark lake closed silently over the broken remains of the House of Usher.

THE CASK OF AMONTILLADO

I plan my revenge

I had been badly treated by Fortunato thousands of times, but I had quietly accepted his ill-treatment. Then, when he started to treat me even worse than before, I decided that I would get my revenge.

You, who know me well, will understand that I did not intend to say anything to anyone about how I would get my revenge. All I knew was that I must get it, there was no doubt of that. I was so sure of this that I knew my plan would have to be perfect, so that it could not go wrong. I must make sure that I punished Fortunato with no risk to myself. It would be no good if I were punished for what I planned to do. But also, Fortunato had to know that I was the one taking revenge on him, or there would be no point in doing it.

Of course, I never once let Fortunato realize that I hated him. He never doubted my friendliness towards him. I continued, as I had always done, to smile at him. He never realized that now I smiled at the thought of what I was going to do.

Fortunato was a man who was respected and feared. But he had one weak point. He considered himself one of the best judges of the quality of wine. Indeed, he was one of the few Italians who really could judge wine. I knew quite a lot too, especially about Italian wines, and I bought a lot whenever I could.

A meeting with Fortunato

One evening, during the Carnival season, I met Fortunato in the street. He was dressed in disguise for the Carnival, as was the custom. He was wearing a tightly-fitting suit of two colours. On his head he had a round cap with bells on. He had been drinking quite heavily, and greeted me warmly. I was pleased to see him too, and shook his hand with great pleasure.

I said to him, 'My dear Fortunato, I am lucky to meet you. You are looking very well today! Listen, Fortunato, today I received a cask of wine. I think it is Amontillado, but I'm not absolutely sure.'

'What? A whole cask of Amontillado? Impossible!'

'I am a bit doubtful too,' I replied, 'and I was silly enough to pay the normal Amontillado price as well. I should have asked your opinion first, I suppose, but I could not find you anywhere. So, I decided to buy it in the hope that it really is Amontillado, because then I shall have a bargain, for Amontillado is very difficult to get these days.'

'Amontillado!'

'I am not absolutely sure.'

'Amontillado!'

'I must find out if it really is. I am on my way now to Luchesi. If anyone can tell me, he can.'

'Luchesi cannot tell Amontillado from sherry wine!'

'Well, some people say that he is as good a judge as you.'

'Come, let us go.'

'Go where?'

'To your wine cellar.'

'No, my friend, I know that you are busy, and I would hate to cause you any trouble.'

'I am not busy. Come.'

'No, my friend. Even if you are not busy, I can see that you are suffering from a dreadful cold. My cellar is terribly damp.'

'I want to go, all the same. My cold is nothing. Amontillado! I'm sure you have been cheated. And as for Luchesi, he cannot tell the difference between sherry and Amontillado.'

In the wine cellar

As he said these words, Fortunato took hold of my arm
and demanded that I lead him to my cellar. I needed no
further encouragement. Holding down my hat so that no
5   one would see me with him, I led him quickly towards
my house.

There were no servants at home. They had all left to
enjoy themselves in the streets. I had told them that I was
going out, and that as it was carnival time, I would not
10 return until the morning. I had given orders that they
should stay in. These orders were enough to make sure
that they would all go out as soon as I myself had gone.

I took two lamps from their place on the shelf. I lit
them and gave one to Fortunato. Then we went together
to the door leading down to the cellar. We had to go down
a long, steep staircase, and I warned my companion to
be careful. At last we came to the bottom and stood   5
together in the huge cellar that was built under my house.
My family had always used this cellar for two purposes.
One was for storing wine. The other was as a tomb. It
had been the custom in our family, for many centuries, to
bury our dead in the cellar under the house.   10

My companion walked unsteadily. The bells on his cap
rang out as he moved.

'The cask,' he said.

'It is further on,' I said. 'Look how damp those walls
are.'   15

He turned towards me, and I could see from his eyes
that he was very drunk.

'How long have you had that cough?' I asked.

My poor friend was coughing badly, and for some
minutes he was unable to answer.   20

'It is nothing,' he said, at last.

'Come,' I said, sternly, 'we must go back. This is bad
for your health. You will be really ill, and I can't allow
that. You are rich, respected, admired and loved. You are
happy, as I once was. You must look after yourself. For   25
me it doesn't matter. We will go back. You will be ill, and
I cannot be responsible for that. Besides, Luchesi will tell
me if the wine is really Amontillado or not.'

'Enough,' he said, 'my cough is not that bad. It will not
kill me. I shall not die of a cough.'   30

'True, true,' I replied. 'I didn't mean to alarm you
unnecessarily. But, you must look after yourself. Let's have
some of this red wine. It will help to keep us from getting
cold.'

I opened a bottle of wine, which had been lying, with   35
many others, on one of the shelves that ran along the
walls.

'Drink,' I said, giving him the bottle.

He raised it to his lips with a smile. He had already had far too much. The bells on his cap rang as he threw back his head to drink.

Then he took my arm again and we continued towards the Amontillado.

'This cellar,' he said, 'is very large.'

'My family, the Montresors,' I replied, 'were a famous family, and there were many of them.'

The wine made his eyes shine, and the bells on his hat rang out. We went further into the cellar. I could feel that the wine was affecting me too. At the end of the section we were now in, there was another smaller area. Its walls had been lined with human bones. They were piled right up to the ceiling. Three of the walls in this part of the cellar had bones piled against them. In the fourth wall there was a hole, about four feet wide and six or seven feet high, with a small dark space beyond it. There seemed to be no reason for this space behind the wall, except that it was the gap between two of the huge supports that held the ceiling up.

Fortunato tried to see into the darkness in front of him, but the weak light from his lamp was not strong enough.

'We go in here,' I said, stepping through the hole in the wall. 'The Amontillado is in here.'

Tied to the wall

My friend stepped unsteadily forward, and I followed impatiently at his heels. In a moment, he had reached the far side of the dark space. He stopped uncertainly, looking rather puzzled. A moment later I had got hold of him so that he could not move. He did not know what was happening.

There were two iron rings, about two feet apart, hanging from a far wall. From one of these, some rope was hanging. It took only seconds to twist the rope around his wrists and to tie him to the iron rings. He was much too surprised to try to stop me. When I had finished, I stepped back through the hole in the wall.

'Put your hand on the wall,' I said, 'you can feel how damp it is. I cannot ask you to leave now, I'm afraid. But I am about to leave you. Before I do that, there is one more thing I want to do for you.'

'But what about the Amontillado?' cried my friend, not yet fully recovered from his astonishment.

'Oh yes,' I said. 'The Amontillado.'

As I said these words, I bent down and began moving the fallen bones. Throwing them to one side, I soon uncovered some bricks and other building materials which I had placed there earlier. I quickly began to close up the opening in the wall.

I had hardly finished laying the first row of bricks when I discovered that Fortunato was becoming less drunk by the second. I realized this because I heard a low cry coming from the dark space. It was not the cry of a drunken man. Then there was a long, long silence. I built the second row of bricks, then the third and the fourth. Then I could hear Fortunato struggling against the rope that tied him to the wall. The noise lasted for several minutes, and I listened to it with growing satisfaction. I even stopped my work for a few minutes so that I could hear more clearly. When at last the noise stopped, I started again. I finished the fifth, the sixth and the seventh rows. The bricks were now nearly level with my chest. I paused again. I took my lamp and held it up. The weak light shone faintly on the figure tied to the wall.

Screams

Suddenly, great screams started to come from the figure tied to the wall. I moved back, surprised and frightened. For a brief moment I trembled. I took my knife from my pocket, struggled over the brick wall, and began to move towards my victim. Then I stopped, and changed my mind. I went back over the wall. I replied to the screams of my victim with screams of my own. Fortunato soon stopped. It was useless. No-one would be able to hear us.

It was now nearly midnight, and my work was almost finished. I had done the eighth, ninth and tenth rows and was doing the last row, the eleventh. There was only one more brick to put into place. I struggled with its weight. I half fitted it into the one remaining place. Then a low laugh came out of the dark space that made the hairs on the back of my head stand up in terror. The laugh was followed by a sad voice, which I hardly recognized as Fortunato's. The voice said:

'Ha! ha! ha! — he! he! A very good joke indeed. An excellent joke. We will have many laughs over it later. He! he! he! We will have many laughs over our wine. He! he! he!'

'The Amontillado!' I said.

'He! he! he! He! he! he! Yes, the Amontillado. But isn't it getting late? Won't our friends be waiting for us? My wife and the rest will be waiting. Let us go. For the love of God, Montresor!'

'Yes,' I said, 'for the love of God!'

I waited for a reply to my words, but none came. I grew impatient. I called aloud:

'Fortunato!'

No answer. I called again:

'Fortunato!'

Still no answer. I lifted up my lamp and its rays shone through the one small, remaining gap. I heard only the ringing of tiny bells. My heart grew sick. I persuaded myself that it was because of the damp in the cellar. I tried to finish my work quickly. I forced the last brick into position. I piled up the bones in their old place against the wall. For half a century, nobody has disturbed them.

Rest in peace, Fortunato, my dear friend!

8

THE STOLEN LETTER

A visit from the Chief of Police

Outside it was a dark, windy evening. I was sitting with my friend Mr Dupin in the library of his house. For at least one hour, we had been sitting in total silence. A stranger,
5 seeing us like that, would have thought that we were only watching the smoke that rose slowly from our pipes. The real truth, though, was quite different. I was thinking about certain subjects that we had discussed earlier. Dupin was so clever that, even when we had finished discussing
10 something, there was always plenty left for me to think about.

Then, quite unexpectedly, there was a knock on the door, and in walked the Chief of the Paris Police.

We welcomed him warmly, for we always found him
15 amusing, even though he was not too clever. I wondered why he had come to Dupin's house, because he had not visited us there for several years.

Dupin rose in order to light a lamp, for we had been sitting in the dark. But before he could do so, the Chief
20 of Police told us he wanted to ask Dupin for advice about some official business, which was causing him a great deal of trouble. When he heard this, Dupin sat down again without bothering to light the lamp. It was always his way to think in the dark. I thought he probably found the
25 darkness helpful. His next words told me that I was right. 'If it is something that requires thought,' said Dupin, 'we shall be able to think better in the dark.'

'That is another of your odd ways,' said the Chief, who had a habit of calling everything 'odd' when he didn't
30 understand it. We believed, therefore, that he must have

lived in a world surrounded by odd things, since he understood very little.

A clear mystery

After the Chief had sat down and made himself comfortable, Dupin asked him what the problem was.

'Well, the fact is,' began the Chief, trying to sound important, 'it's really a very simple thing indeed. I'm quite sure we can solve it by ourselves, but I thought that Dupin would like to hear the facts about this business because the whole thing is so very odd.'

'Simple and odd,' said Dupin.

'Why, yes, but not exactly that either. The fact is, we have all been rather puzzled because it looks so simple.'

'Perhaps it is the simplicity of the thing which is causing the trouble,' said my friend.

'What nonsense you talk!' replied the Chief, laughing loudly.

'Perhaps the mystery is a little too clear,' said Dupin.

'Oh, Good Heavens! A clear mystery! Whoever heard of such a thing?' The Chief laughed even louder than before.

'Well, what is this problem you want to talk about?' I asked, a little impatiently.

'I will tell you,' replied the Chief. 'I will tell you in a few words, but before I begin, I must warn you that this matter is secret. I would probably lose my job if it were known that I had told anyone about it.'

'Well, start then,' I said.

'But if you would rather not …' said Dupin.

'Well, then,' said the Chief, taking no notice of Dupin, and starting at last. 'I have received information from a royal person, that a document of great importance has been stolen from the palace. The person who stole the document is definitely known. He was seen taking it. It is also known that he still has the document.'

'How is this known?' asked Dupin.

'It is known,' replied the Chief, 'because of what the document is, and because certain things have not happened which would immediately happen if the robber no longer had the document. In other words, the only way the robber can use this document is to give it to a third person, whom we shall not name, and then we would immediately know that he no longer had it.'

'Please be a little clearer,' I said.

'Well, let me say that the paper gives this robber a certain power in a certain place where such power is very valuable.' The Chief never liked to give exact details.

'I still do not quite understand,' said Dupin.

'No? Well, showing this document to the third person would cause great difficulties for the royal person. This is what gives the robber such power over this person.'

'But this must mean,' I interrupted, 'that the person who had the document in the first place, must know who took it. In other words, the person who will be in difficulties, knows who the robber is. But who would dare —'

The Minister has the letter

'The robber,' said the Chief, 'is Minister Devine, who dares to do many things, some good, some bad. Minister Devine took the document cleverly and boldly. This document, which is a letter, had been sent to the royal person in her private rooms. While she was reading it, she was suddenly interrupted by the third person, who is a very important person, from whom she knew she must keep the letter a secret. She tried to hide it in a drawer, but did not have time. In the end she had to place it, open, on the top of the table. However, the contents of the letter could not be seen, only the address.

'At this point, Minister Devine came into the room. He immediately saw the letter and recognized the handwriting. He also noticed the confusion of the lady and realized what her secret was. After he completed the purpose of his visit, he brought out a letter rather similar to the one on the table. He opened it, pretended to read it, and then placed it next to the other one. He continued to talk for a little while about ordinary matters. At last he decided to go, taking from the table the lady's letter, not his own. The lady saw what he was doing, but of course she did not dare to say so because the very important person was standing next to her. The Minister left, leaving his own unimportant letter on the table.'

'Ah, I see,' said Dupin to me. 'We now know how the Minister has achieved his power over the lady. He knows that the lady knows that he took the letter.'

'Yes,' replied the Chief of Police, 'and he has been using that power for a number of months. The lady who was robbed knows how necessary it is to get her letter back, but she does not know how to do it. In the end, she decided that the best thing to do was to tell me all about it.'

'It is clear,' I said, 'that the Minister still has the letter, since it is the possession of the letter that gives him his power. Once he uses the letter, his power will end.'

'That is true,' said the Chief, 'and I believe it. The first thing I had to do, then, was to make a careful search of the Minister's house. The difficulty here was how to search the house without the Minister knowing, for I had been warned that it would be dangerous if he ever learnt of what I intended to do.'

'But,' I interrupted, 'you know how to do these things. The police in Paris are always searching people's homes.'

Fools and poets

'Oh yes, so I was not too worried. Indeed, the Minister's habits helped a great deal. He is often away from home all night. He does not have many servants. They sleep quite a long way from their master's rooms. My men easily made them drunk, and I have keys, as you know, that will open any door in Paris.

'I searched that house every night for three months. I went there myself, for it is important work, and the reward is huge. I did not stop the search until I was absolutely sure that the thief was a cleverer man than myself. I must have searched every possible place in which he could have hidden that letter.'

'But, isn't it possible that although the Minister has the letter,' I said, 'he might have hidden it somewhere else?'

'I doubt that,' said Dupin. 'With the kind of political power that the Minister has now, the letter needs to be somewhere where he can get it at any time, quickly and easily. That is almost as important as having the letter.'

'True,' I said. 'Therefore the letter must be in his house somewhere. He cannot carry it around with him.'

'That's right,' said the Chief. 'We know he does not carry it with him. We have attacked him twice and searched his clothes. No doubt he thought that the men who attacked him were ordinary thieves. Anyway, they found nothing.'

'That was rather unnecessary,' said Dupin. 'I know that the Minister is not a fool, and he must have realized that something like that would happen.'

'Not altogether a fool,' said the Chief, 'but he is a poet as well as a politician, and I have always thought that fools and poets are very similar.'

'Perhaps you are right,' said Dupin, after a long thoughtful pause. 'Although I write poetry myself.'

'Why don't you tell us,' I said to the Chief quickly, 'exactly how and what you searched?'

The search

'Well, we searched through the Minister's home slowly and carefully. We looked everywhere, I tell you. I know how to do this kind of thing. We went through the whole place, room by room. We took five nights to search each room. First we searched the furniture. We opened every possible drawer, and I am sure you know that it is impossible to hide a secret drawer from a trained policeman. We know that there is a certain amount of space in any piece of furniture. We measure it carefully, and if there is more space than there are drawers, there must be a secret drawer, and so we find it. There were none. Then we searched the chairs, and we even took the tops off the tables.'

'Why did you do that?' I asked.

'Sometimes the top of a table is removed by a person wishing to hide something. He then makes a hole in the leg of the table and hides whatever it is he wishes to hide, in that hole. He then replaces the top, and it looks as if everything is normal. The legs of beds can be used in the same way.'

'But you could not have taken all the pieces of furniture apart in this way. Anyway, what about the chairs? If the letter was rolled up tightly enough, it could be hidden in the leg of a chair. You didn't take apart all the chairs, did
5   you?' said Dupin.

'Certainly not. We did better. We examined every chair in the house, in fact we examined all the furniture. If there had been any signs of someone taking the furniture apart, we would have noticed. For example, if there had been
10 new glue or any scratches made in the past few days, we would have seen them.'

'I suppose you looked at the mirrors, the beds, the bedclothes, as well as the curtains and carpets.'

'Of course we did. When we had looked at every piece
15 of furniture in the ways I have told you, we examined the house itself. We even searched the two neighbouring houses.'

'The two neighbouring houses!' I exclaimed. 'You have been to a great deal of trouble.'

'We have, but the reward offered is huge.'
20 'You looked among the Minister's papers, of course, and examined his books in the library?'

'Of course. We opened every package and parcel. We opened every book, and turned every page. We measured the thickness of every book cover and made sure that
25 nothing had been hidden in them.'

'You examined the floors under the carpets?'

'Yes, we did, and the walls, and the cellar.'

'Well,' I said, 'you must have been mistaken about the letter being in the Minister's home. It cannot be there.'
30 'I'm afraid you must be right,' said the Chief. 'And now, Dupin, what do you advise me to do?'

'To search the house again, carefully.'

'That is absolutely unnecessary. I am quite sure that the letter is not there.'
35 'I cannot offer you any better advice than that,' said Dupin. 'You have, of course, an accurate description of the letter?'

'Oh yes!' The Chief of Police at once took out his notebook and read out to us a detailed description of the missing document.

As soon as he had done this, he left. I had never seen him look so worried and upset before.   5

The Chief of Police makes a promise

About a month later, the Chief of Police visited us again. He sat down with us and took out his pipe. We talked of a number of different things for a short time. At last I said, 'Well then, what has been happening about that stolen   10 letter?'

'Well, I made another search, as Dupin suggested,' the Chief answered, 'but it was no use. I knew it wouldn't be.'

'How much did you say the reward was?' asked Dupin.   15

'A lot of money. I don't like to say how much exactly, but I will say that I would give 50,000 francs to anyone who could get the letter for me. The fact is, it is becoming more and more important every day, and the reward has been doubled. But even if it were three times as much, I   20 could not do any more than I have already done.'

'Well,' said Dupin, 'if you promise to pay me the sum of 50,000 francs, which you said you would give to anyone who could get the letter for you, then I will give you the letter.'   25

I was amazed. The Chief of Police looked equally astonished. For some minutes he remained speechless and absolutely still. Then he recovered. He took out a pen from his pocket and asked Dupin for some paper. He then wrote that he promised to pay Dupin the sum   30 of 50,000 francs. He handed the paper to Dupin. Dupin examined what he had written carefully, and put the piece of paper in his jacket pocket. Then, unlocking a drawer in his desk, he took out the letter and gave it to the Chief.   35

The Chief of the Paris police was delighted. He opened the letter with a shaking hand, looked quickly at the contents, and then rushed out of the house. He did not even take the time to say 'Thank you' and wish us goodbye.

When he had gone, my friend explained what had happened.

'The Paris police,' he said, 'are very good in their own way. They try hard and have been well trained to do their duty. Therefore, when the Chief told us how they had searched the Minister's house, I felt sure they had in fact searched it very well and carefully, so far as they knew how.'

'So far as they knew how?' I said.

'Yes,' said Dupin. 'The methods they used were not only the best of their kind, but they were followed properly. If the letter had been where they searched they would definitely have found it.'

I only laughed, but Dupin seemed quite serious about what he was saying.

The cleverness of Minister Devine

'The only mistake of the police was that these methods should not have been applied to this case nor to this Minister. The Chief of Police and his men searched only in the places that they thought of as hiding places. They did not realize that they were dealing with a much cleverer person than themselves.

'The Chief of Police always makes the mistake of thinking either too deeply or too simply about a problem. Many schoolboys use their heads better than he does. Once I knew a boy about eight years old, who was very successful in the game of "Even or Odd". This game is simple and is played with stones. One player holds in his hand a number of these stones. He asks another boy to guess whether he is holding an even or an odd number of stones. If the guess is right, the boy who guesses correctly wins one stone. If he is wrong, he loses one. The boy I am speaking about was so successful at guessing, that he won all the stones in the school. Of course, he had a method of guessing. He was always able to observe and to measure the cleverness of the others.

'When I asked the boy how he was always so successful, he replied to me as follows, "When I wish to find out how wise, or how stupid, or how good someone is, or what he is thinking, I make the expression on my face appear the same as the expression of the other person. Then I wait to see what ideas come into my head."

'What the Chief of Police does is to consider only his own clever ideas. He does not think of what the criminal is thinking. The Chief of Police is successful if the mind of the criminal is the same as his own mind, but if the criminal is cleverer, then the Chief of Police will probably fail.

'Now I know the Minister, and I knew that he would use no ordinary hiding place. He knew everything would be searched very carefully. I am sure that he expected his house to be searched, and that he left it empty on purpose. I expect he thought that once the police had had the chance to search the place carefully, they would be certain that the letter was not there. This, in fact, is exactly what happened. I decided that the Minister would have thought of all this, and so, in order to hide the letter from the police, he would have used simplicity. You remember, perhaps, how much the Chief of Police laughed, the first time he came here, about the stolen letter? He was laughing because I suggested to him that a possible reason why he could not solve the mystery was because it was probably so clear.'

'Yes,' I said, 'I remember that well. I thought he looked very foolish.'

'Our dear Chief never once thought,' continued Dupin, 'that the Minister might have placed the letter right out in the open, under the nose of the whole world. What better

place could there be to put something that you wanted no one to notice? Well, the more I thought about the cleverness of the Minister, the more I was sure I was right. The document had to be near him at all times, or it would
5 be useless.

'I therefore made up my mind that I would visit the Minister myself. I bought a pair of dark green glasses just before I called at his home. I found the Minister in his library, looking very bored, though in fact he only
10 pretends to be bored. He wants people to believe there is nothing to fear about him.

'I pretended something myself that day. I told him of my weak eyes, and how much I disliked the fact that I had to wear glasses. But even as I was telling him this, I
15 was looking very carefully around the room.

'I paid special attention to a large writing table where he was sitting. It was quite untidy, with a lot of papers lying about on top of it. However, after I had looked at everything there, I was certain that the letter was not
20 among those papers.'

The letter is seen

'I looked around the whole room, and at last I saw a small open box above the fireplace. The box was divided into sections. I could see five or six visiting cards and a letter.
25 This last object was very dirty and bent. It was torn nearly in half across the middle, as if the Minister had decided to tear it up because it was worthless, and then changed his mind. It was clearly addressed, in a woman's handwriting, to the Minister himself.

30 'As soon as I saw this letter, I was sure that it was the one that I was looking for. I knew that it looked very different from the description that the Chief of Police gave us, but that did not matter. It was so dirty and torn, and so clearly addressed to the wrong person that I felt it was
35 too different, and I was suspicious.

'I stayed there as long as I could, talking about a subject that I knew interested him, but all the time I was really studying the letter. Then I discovered something that made any doubts I had about the letter vanish. I realized that the envelope had been folded inside out. I then said   5
goodbye to the Minister and left, leaving my keys on the table.'

Dupin takes the letter

'The next morning I called to collect my keys, which luckily were not important ones, and we continued the   10
discussion we had had the day before. While
we were talking, we heard a loud noise,
like a gun-shot, coming from the
street. This was followed by
a lot of screaming
and shouting.

'The Minister rushed to
the window and looked out. In the
meantime, I stepped up to the box above
the fireplace, took the letter, and put it in my pocket. I   20
replaced it with another, almost the same, which I had
brought with me.

'The trouble in the street had been caused by a man
firing a gun into a crowd of women and children.
However it seemed that the gun had not been loaded and   25

he had done no harm. Once that was realized, the noise and bother soon stopped. When everything quietened down, the Minister left the window. I had moved to join him there as soon as I had taken the letter. Soon afterwards, I said goodbye. The man who had fired the gun in the street was, of course, employed by me.'

'But why,' I asked, 'did you replace the letter with another? Wouldn't it have been better just to have taken the letter you wanted and then left?'

'The Minister,' said Dupin, 'might have killed me if he had guessed what I had done. I doubt that I would have left his house alive. But I had another reason, apart from my own safety. For eighteen months he has had a lovely lady in his power. She now has him in her power. Because he does not realize that he no longer has the letter, he will continue to behave as though he has, and he will therefore bring about his own ruin.

'I would very much like to know his thoughts and read his mind when he is forced to open that letter in front of the "royal person" the Chief of Police told us about.'

Dupin's message

There was still one thing that I wanted to know about. 'As a matter of interest,' I said, 'what was in the letter that you left behind?'

'Well, it did not seem right to leave the envelope empty, so I decided to put down a line from one of my own poems,' laughed Dupin. 'Minister Devine once did me an evil deed when we were both in London, and I told him then that I would get my revenge one day. So, as I knew that he would want to know who had stopped his evil plan, I decided to give him a clue. He has read my poems, I know, so he will recognize the words I wrote:

A plan so terrible is not worthy of a man so powerful.'

QUESTIONS AND ACTIVITIES

CHAPTER 1

Use these words to fill in the gaps: **wildly, underground, judges, opened, straight, rushing, awaited, buried, carefully, everlasting, pushed, result, fainted, directions, terrified.**

When I (1) _____ my eyes, the blackness of (2) _____ night closed in around me. A fearful idea suddenly sent the blood (3) _____ to my head, and I (4) _____ again. When I recovered, I (5) _____ out my arms (6) _____ above and around me in all (7) _____. I was (8) _____ to move in case I went (9) _____ into a wall. I thought that they might have (10) _____ me alive (11) _____. I stepped (12) _____ forward. Whatever it was that (13) _____ me, I knew my (14) _____ well enough to feel sure that the (15) _____ would be death.

CHAPTER 2

Put these sentences in the right order to say what the story is about. Start with number 9.

1 The cat nearly made me trip down the steep stairs.
2 Now when the cat heard me coming, he ran away in fear.
3 She fell dead at my feet; I had murdered my wife.
4 The day after, I saw the shape of a huge cat on my wall.
5 My wife tried to stop me, so I buried the axe in her head.
6 I took it into my house, but I soon began to hate the cat.
7 His obvious dislike made me so angry that I hanged him.
8 One day my wife and I both went down to the cellar.
9 One night Pluto scratched my hand, so I cut out his eye.
10 Then a black cat followed me home from a restaurant.
11 That night my house was destroyed by a fire.
12 I was so angry that I raised my axe to hit the animal.

CHAPTER 3 (A)

Match the witnesses to the evidence they gave.

1 **The washerwoman**
   (a) 'I heard a Frenchman speak in a harsh voice.'
2 **The tobacco shop owner**
   (b) 'I forced the door open with an iron bar.'
3 **The policeman**
   (c) 'I went with Mrs Spain to her house that day at noon.'
4 **The silver merchant**
   (d) 'The ladies seemed very friendly towards each other.'
5 **The restaurant owner**
   (e) 'She asked for 4,000 francs, which I paid in gold.'
6 **The bank manager**
   (f) 'The high voice could have been a German woman's.'
7 **The bank clerk**
   (g) 'They had lived there for more than six years.'
8 **The tailor**
   (h) 'I believe the high voice was that of an Italian.'

CHAPTER 3 (B)

Correct the fourteen errors in the sailor's story.

I captured the orang-utan in China, and brought it to my home in London. Late one afternoon the animal escaped and I followed it. It climbed up a tree into Mrs Spain's window. The ladies were sitting facing the window. It seized the daughter, and with two sweeps of its arm it nearly cut her head from her body. The sight of blood made the ape very quiet. It picked up the old lady by the hair, but then saw at the window the horrified face of a policeman. It was at once angry. It seized the body of the daughter and pushed it under the bed. Then it pushed the old lady straight up the chimney.

CHAPTER 4

Put the letters of these words in the right order.

I was (1) **zadema** when I met Mrs Wyatt. To me, she appeared to be quite a (2) **nilpa** woman. She was, however, very (3) **lewl**

sreddes. She was (4) **lyndifer**, and talked quite (5) **pailphy** with all the other ladies. I was rather (6) **hoidentass**, for I had heard that she was very (7) **verlce**. The (8) **thurt** was that people often (9) **guelahd** at her. The ladies thought she was not (10) **etrypt**, totally (11) **nucedutade**, and rather stupid. I (12) **drewoden** how Wyatt had been (13) **paptred** into (14) **gnarmiry** such a person.

CHAPTER 5

Which of these sentences are true? What is wrong with the false ones?

1 The mummy was in a box, nearly eight feet in length.
2 The body was in the third case, wrapped in bandages.
3 It was in excellent condition, and did not smell.
4 We passed electric currents through the mummy.
5 It drew up its left knee and gave Dr Ponnonner a kick.
6 Then it opened its eyes, sneezed, sat up, and spoke.
7 We were all very frightened by these odd happenings.
8 The mummy was eager to continue the experiments.
9 He said that he was only just over 700 years old.
10 The people of his time had no medical knowledge.

CHAPTER 6 (A)

The (b) sentences are all in the wrong place. Which paragraphs should they go in?

1 (a) When I saw the House of Usher, it made me feel very uneasy. (b) I watched him closely. (c) The plants and trees surrounding it looked unhealthy and lifeless.
2 (a) Roderick told me his illness had always been a family evil. (b) The illness had puzzled her doctors. (c) He felt he was fighting against a 'thing' he could only call 'fear'.
3 (a) Lady Madeline had been very ill for a long time. (b) It seemed cold and unfriendly. (c) She had steadily become weaker and weaker.
4 (a) I spent all my time trying to cheer up my friend. (b) It made him very nervous. (c) I could see that his condition was one of terrible despair.

CHAPTER 6 (B)

Choose the right ending for each sentence.

1 About a week later, the narrator's terror grew because (a) Usher's strange behaviour affected him; (b) his room was strange and dark; (c) he heard terrible, low sounds.

2 The narrator thought there was something different about Usher because (a) he was very pale; (b) he looked full of real joy; (c) his eyes had the light of madness in them.

3 Usher said he was driven mad because (a) his sister was alive when he put her in the cellar; (b) he felt that he was trapped in the house; (c) he did not dare to speak.

4 Usher died because (a) his sister fell on him and killed him; (b) he was a victim of the house's terrors; (c) a crack stretched through the house and the walls fell down.

CHAPTER 7

*Which people do the underlined words refer to: **Montresor**, **Fortunato** or **Luchesi**?*

Montresor wanted to get (1) his revenge. (2) He wanted to punish Fortunato without being punished himself, but (3) he also wanted (4) him to know that (5) he was the person doing it. Fortunato did not know that Montresor hated (6) him.

Montresor told Fortunato (7) he was going to ask Luchesi about some Amontillado (8) he had bought. Fortunato said (9) he did not know much about wine. Montresor said some people thought (10) he was as good a judge as Fortunato.

Montresor pretended that (11) he didn't want to ask Fortunato to come down to (12) his cellar, but Fortunato took (13) his arm and made (14) him lead (15) him to it. In this way (16) he fell into Montresor's trap.

CHAPTER 8

Choose the right answers.

A letter had been stolen from the (1) **palace/police**. Minister Devine was the (2) **royal person/robber**. He kept the letter to obtain power over a (3) **lady/politician**. The Chief of the Paris Police had to get the letter back before the Minister (4) **hid it/showed it to someone**. The Chief had ordered his men to search the Minister's (5) **office/house**. They had been there for the past three (6) **months/weeks**. They had even pretended to be (7) **thieves/soldiers** and had attacked the Minister (8) **once/twice** in order to search though his (9) **library/clothes**. Nothing had been found, and the Chief asked Dupin for his (10) **advice/description**. Dupin said he should search the house again, but this time he should do it (11) **carefully/quickly**.

WHOLE BOOK

Copy the table and fill in the answers. The name of a writer will appear in the centre column.

Who or what …

1 … was thought to be a wine expert?

2 … hissed like the devil as it moved?

3 … tried to shave and then ran away?

4 … packed his wife in salt before sailing?

5 … wanted revenge?

6 … sailed a few days late and lost his ship?

7 … died of a mysterious illness?

8 … loved his master but lost an eye?

9 … was killed by a large animal (Mrs _____)?

10 … hid something in the open?

11 … could think best in the dark?

12 … was kicked through a window?

13 … died of terror?

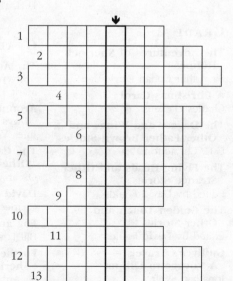